PODCASTING MADE SIMPLE

THE STEP BY STEP GUIDE ON HOW TO START A
SUCCESSFUL PODCAST FROM THE GROUND UP

DANIEL LARSON

AT PUBLISHING

COPYRIGHT

professional before attempting any techniques outlined in this book.

By reading this document, the reader agrees that under no circumstances is the author responsible for any losses, direct or indirect, which are incurred as a result of the use of the information contained within this document, including, but not limited to, errors, omissions, or inaccuracies.

CONTENTS

A SPECIAL OPPORTUNITY

Due to popular demand, I compiled a comprehensive 16-part video training series on how to optimize your show for growth and improve your podcast marketing through simple yet effective strategies.

The crash course takes podcasters from confused and uncertain to clear and confident on how to gain more listeners and grow their audience. As a valued reader of my book, you can access the *Podcast Marketing Kickstarter* with an 80% discount at:

https://daniel-larson.com/reader-special-offer

INTRODUCTION

Podcasting is the rewarding medium we've been missing for decades that allows you to discuss your passions, share your message with the world, and have a massive impact on people's lives. With more than 6.5 million weekly listeners in the UK and over 72 million weekly listeners in the United States, there are literally millions of people waiting for you to impact their lives with your message. Additionally, podcasting is a trending business model that carries as much bite as it does bark. The fact that more than half of listeners are interested in buying products they learned about through a podcast, renders it a hobby with a highly profitable potential.

The fact that you are here proves that I don't need to sell the idea of podcasting to you. You have already decided that you want to start podcasting. Now, you are looking for details on how to do it! Fortunately, *Podcasting Made Simple* contains everything you need to get started.

There are many reasons why you may be interested in starting a podcast right now. You may desire to build a passionately engaged audience that is inspired by what you talk about, just as much as you are. Even if you are not entirely sure of what that passion is yet, you

can feel in your heart that there is something worth talking about that is longing for your attention, and capable of having a huge impact on your listeners. Or, you may have an idea of a podcast that should exist but doesn't yet, so you want to be the one to get it to market. Maybe, your number one focus here is to market your exist ing business or create a brand new business through your podcast that will earn you an incredible profit. No matter what your reason ing is, you can be sure that podcasting is a great way to fulfil your needs and that you will discover exactly how to do that right here.

In this book, I'm removing every inch of uncertainty from your experience so that you know the exact steps to take to create your podcast and reach all of your podcasting goals, every single time. With the steps I share, you can develop your own professionally produced, highly captivating show that nurtures your passion for sharing while capturing the attention of listeners everywhere.

The comprehensive guides inside *Podcasting Made Simple* will cover everything from creating a viable plan for your podcast, branding and marketing your podcast, what equipment you need for the best sound and experience, how to edit, produce, and share your podcast, and more. Even if you are not particularly outgoing, you will discover how to find your unique voice and share it with the world through your podcast. Each chapter is full of specific strategies and instructions that will help you minimize the hurdles and launch your podcast into success in minimal timing. You will discover that, although this can be a business model, podcasting is a fun experience that can bring a lot of joy to your life. I, myself, have experienced the magnificent joy of sharing my own passion through pod casts, and I can vouch that there is something so wonderful about being able to show up, talk about something you love, and experience the fascination of everyone who listens to your show on a regular basis.

Over recent years, I have grown to love and care for the ever passionate podcast community. Despite the growing size and popularity of podcasts, very few guides exist that go into great detail about the specifics around creating a highly successful and profitable podcast. I want to change that. I want to provide you with an excellent launch pad so that you can take your enthusiastic beginner's mentality and turn it into your own ultimate success story. My goal here is to pro vide you with specific action steps you can take, free of any contradictory information, and thoroughly researched so that you know you are doing everything it takes to generate a successful podcast. Whether you want to have a solo podcast, a talk show, or a hand over-fist profitable business model, you will discover everything you need to generate success right here in *Podcasting Made Simple.*

I must admit, writing this book is as much for my pleasure as it is for your benefit. Over the past years, I have become obsessed with find ing new, innovative ways to develop a podcast, as well as under standing tested and respected methods that get results. Having an outlet for me to put this all together while developing a cohesive and comprehensive guide for you has been a blast for me. I hope you will find it to be a great asset for you as you take on the exciting process of creating, recording, publishing, and promoting your podcast.

I suggest you read this book over ten days, reading one chapter per day, so you can fully absorb all of the valuable information here in this book. The more you understand the secrets of brilliant podcasts, and all of the steps that go into making one, the easier it will be for you to turn your podcast into a great success. By the end, you will have an excellent understanding of what it takes to develop a successful podcast from start to finish. This way, not only are you aware of what you need to do, but you also understand how and you can feel confident in achieving your goals through a simple step-by-step process.

It is important that you understand that podcasting can be highly profitable, but it is not a get-rich-quick scheme. You must be willing to take the necessary action to turn it into a success and push your self to reach all of your goals. If you do, however, you can make an incredible profit off of your podcast. Not only that, but you can also take your entire brand and transform it into multiple profit streams, effectively growing your income-producing abilities. Once you have an established audience, money *can* be made, and you can achieve financial stability through your podcast. The trick is, you have to genuinely love what you are doing and be willing to do it without any revenue coming from it, as this level of joy ensures that you have the passion and devotion required to turn a profit. With this deep level of commitment to something you love, you will have the energy to show up with passion and consistency, enough so that your audience stays engaged. When your engaged audience begins to form, the opportunity for earning an income starts.

After years of researching podcasts of all sizes, and investing time in understanding the ins and outs of what it takes to develop a successful podcast, I am confident that I can show you the way to success with your own podcast. The methods I unveil to you in this book have been used by the most successful podcasters who are both profitable and wildly in love with the work they do and work in a low-stress way.

If you implement everything instructed to you in this guide, you will be able to turn your podcasting vision into a reality. Whether your goal is big or small, you will be able to transform it into an enriching journey that amplifies your life in many ways. This book is the most well-informed source of information to guide you to make the best decisions that will best serve you and your audience through your podcast. You already know this is something you want to do, so now you have to put your head down and make it happen. With podcasting, you truly will get out what you put in, so don't let your dreams remain idle ideas that stay untouched in the depths of your mind. Release them, research them, and turn them into your reality. The time is now.

In case you are worried about being late to the podcasting party, I want to assure you that you are not. You have made it just in the nick of time! However, podcasting is a rapidly growing medium, and thousands of new podcasts are popping up every single day. Everyone wants to have their share of success in the podcasting world, while also getting to have a say on the things they are most passionate about! If you really want to strike it large, you must not put it off. You must start developing your podcast right away and get it to market as soon as possible. The quicker you are to jump into action now, the larger your podcast will be. The longer you wait, the more saturated the market gets, the quieter your voice gets amongst the thousand others and the more challenging it becomes to climb your way to the top. Let everyone else sleep on this incredible opportunity while *you* become one of the ones who made it happen.

Action is the first step in reaching your goals, so buckle up; you're about to start a thrilling journey that will transform your life. Let's begin!

1

ENVISIONING THE DREAM AND KNOWING WHY

I f you are not already convinced, podcasting is an incredible medium to get into. The unique power of a podcast is that it captures your audience's attention, creates a unique and personalized connection between yourself and your audience, and connects you with your audience at any time. Unlike blogs or videos, where your audience must have time to actively read or watch your content, podcasts can be consumed on-the-go. As you likely already know, our modern world is all about *go*.

Aside from fitting your business into their busy schedules, podcast ing gives you the opportunity to provide an abundance of benefits to your audience. You can offer entertainment, education, interviews, or any other number of unique listener experiences that provide your audience with a wonderful reason to tune in for every episode. Truly, there are many great ways that you can benefit your audience through the power of your podcast.

Your audience isn't the only one benefitting from your podcast, though. Although you may be creating your podcast for your audience, and promoting it so that you can connect with your audience, there are many benefits that you stand to gain from your podcast, too. One great value you gain from your podcast is offered in the form of therapeutic value. Therapeutic values such as learning to be come a better individual through giving people a voice, feeling a sense of personal accomplishment for something you put together yourself, and being able to express yourself and your thoughts all have highly therapeutic values. The level of pride you feel in your self as you celebrate your own successes is wonderful for your self esteem, self-confidence, and overall sense of self-worth.

Another benefit you gain from your podcast is known as a parasocial relationship. Parasocial relationships are one-sided relationships that form between media personas and their audiences. The easiest way to understand a parasocial relationship is to consider a media persona you adore, such as a singer, actor or actress, or other media personality. Now, consider the way you feel about that person. Chances are, you feel like you have some form of meaningful connection with them, despite the fact that they have no idea who you are. Still, be cause you are a part of their overall audience, they care about you and add to the relationship, just not on a personal level. Parasocial relationships can be healthy to an extent, offering a sense of belong ing and creating a wonderful sense of community. However, it is important that you do not rely exclusively on parasocial relation-ships in your life, or you will begin to feel lonely and disconnected from the world around you. As you grow, continue to nurture interpersonal relationships you develop through your podcast. This will not only support you with growing your podcast but developing your sense of wellbeing, too.

Before you can tap into all of these benefits you and your audience both gain, you must know *why* you are here building your podcast in the first place. What specifically has drawn you to podcasting, and why is this such an important dream of yours? What about this dream makes it worth pursuing, and how are you going to use this to compel you to keep going? The answer is in the details...

One of the biggest mistakes new podcasters, or business owners in general, can make is failing to clearly define what their dream is and why they want that dream. Without these two elements, you are set ting yourself up for failure. A dream gives you a clear sense of direction and a tangible measuring stick to monitor your results with, while a reason why gives you the fuel you need to reach those results and fulfill your inevitable dream.

To define your dream requires a two-pronged approach. You must first let yourself go, free of any expectations, to write down every thing you truly want for your podcast. At this point, you want to imagine that your podcast is already a massive success and that it has become everything you hoped it would be and more. Use this imaginative game to define what success looks like for you. Be as specific as you possibly can, as details help drive success. Vague statements like "I make $10,000 a month and people like me" are not going to provide you with a clear vision to work toward. If anything, these indecisive statements will actually drive you away from putting effort in because it leads to you feeling overwhelmed by the statement you have made, and confused with how to proceed. Rather than giving you an "open-ended dream to run toward," it ends up boxing you in, making you feel like there is no point trying because your dream is too big to achieve.

Instead, try creating statements like "I easily earn $10,000 through advertisements, sponsorships, and affiliate marketing deals, and I feel relaxed and confident doing it. My followers are engaged, enjoy listening to me, and contribute to the community that I am building through my podcast with their own anecdotes, willingness to participate, and loyalty to listening." Dream about what your studio will look like, where your podcast will be produced, and what it will feel like to vocalize your opinion on things you are passionate about. Consider the relationship you share with your audience, what it will be like, and how fun it will be to partake in that relationship with the people who are following you. Even allow yourself to dream of your brand, and how your brand will represent you and your podcast, and come to be a point of excitement for your audience.

If you already know what you want to speak about, you can also write down what you want to speak about in a specific manner. Again, do not be vague about this. Get clear on what your podcast will be about, and how your podcast will benefit your listeners. Understand what value you will be giving them and how this value will transform their life. These specific statements are invaluable when it comes to launching your own podcast, starting with a crystal-clear dream.

If you do not yet know what you want to talk about, see if you can define what it will feel like to be producing content for your podcast. Do you want to feel inspired? Passionate? Entertained? Intrigued? Curious? Mysterious? Define what the content will feel like, how it will feel creating it, and how that fits into your overall vision of having a podcast.

I cannot stress enough the importance of being specific throughout this entire process. The clearer you can be when dreaming up these early stages, the easier your podcast development will be because you have a clear sense of direction and focus. The value you gain here is immeasurable, as it truly will direct you straight toward your success. Imagine giving yourself a literal roadmap to where you are going. Rather than giving vague directions like "head west for twenty minutes, then turn slightly south," give yourself clear directions. Your specific description creates a specific set of guidelines and a clear destination, and as a result, you are far more likely to actually get there.

After you have defined your dream in broad terms, the second step is to quickly compare your dream to a S.M.A.R.T goal. S.M.A.R.T goals are the most powerful goals you can develop, as they truly turn your plans into a measurable destination that you can use to drive your actions. Always transform any dream into a smart goal before attempting to fulfill said dream, as this will make it far more attainable. To compare your dream to a S.M.A.R.T goal, you need to make sure it is Specific, Measurable, Attainable, Realistic, and Timed, or able to be given a deadline for when you want to achieve it by. If you can see these five elements defined in your dream, you have an excellent foundation to launch from.

Knowing where you need to go is crucial, but having the fuel to get there is equally as important. After all, it does not matter if you know where you need to go if you have absolutely no fuel to get you there. It is true for a road trip, and it is true for your podcast, too! The fuel to this whole experience is your desire, resiliency, strength, courage, and willingness. In the business, we call it your "why." In other words, why are you even doing this? Knowing why you are doing something, and having a truly meaningful reason for doing it, enables you to motivate yourself and keep your energy up as you work through the process of getting yourself to your dreams. Without a clear, meaningful reason behind why you are doing something, you will surely give up the second things look challenging or seem to require more energy or effort than you have to give them. In any industry, the most successful people all have a clear reason for their actions. They know that this clear reason is the most important thing because without it they never get anywhere. With it, they get everywhere.

Defining your why is a process that must be highly personal to you. You must know exactly what matters to you, what has the power to move you and drive you, and what is going to get you going even when times get challenging. Most times, people with great success decide to turn their why from a "what?" into a "who?" In other words, it's not what they're working toward; it's who they're doing it for that matters most. Marathon runners, for example, run for the people they love by dedicating their races to them, which gives them the energy and strength to keep going. This is the secret to really giving yourself a reason that is beyond powerful, and that will keep you going all the way until you reach your dreams and beyond.

See, people who go after a "what" instead of a "who" often attach their meaningful association to something that is not particularly responsive, or worthy of pursuing. A major driving factor many people believe they have is money, for example. You might think that the reason why you want to do something is money. Perhaps you have decided you want to be a six-figure income earner, or a millionaire, or even a multi-millionaire. The thing is, though, money is non reciprocated. You will work hard for your money, and your money will fluctuate. Sometimes it is there; sometimes, it is not there. Some times it is easy to come by, sometimes it eludes you, and you cannot seem to get your hands on any. Even if you do have a lot and you master maintaining high levels of money, money will not keep you company, behave like a friend, or offer you anything beyond financial security and opportunity. While it may seem worthwhile at first, the reality is that money is a fickle lover, and so it should be seen more as a by-product or a part of the motivator, and not *the* driving "why" itself.

The same goes for financial security, the house of your dreams, the city of your dreams, the vacations you long for, the wardrobe you think will make you happy, or anything else that exists in the material world. A material desire will always let you down because the moment you acquire it, the emotional drive is gone. While you may continue to appreciate it and be fond of it, the novelty wears off, the emotional high disappears, and you are left by yourself looking for that next emotional high in yet another material item. As soon as you fulfill your next emotional high, you will be left feeling unfulfilled all over again. The sense of fulfillment from material goods will always be finite and quick to drain. Never motivate yourself with these, as you will struggle to maintain your motivation and keep going, which can drastically reduce your momentum and your success.

A more powerful way to motivate yourself and a way that is deeply engraved in the medium of podcasting is to motivate yourself with a "who." Your "who" might be someone in your life that you love very much, someone who you have yet to meet, or the very people you want to represent with your podcast. Make sure that whoever you choose is important to you and will continue to motivate you, even in challenging times.

When you associate your "why" with a living being, you become far more likely to achieve your why because you experience a powerful, sustainable, and fulfilling back-and-forth exchange of emotions that drives you. For example, if you start a podcast because you want to give a voice to an underrepresented part of your community, the relationships you build within that community will flourish and thrive through your efforts. As a result, you will receive positive emotional fulfillment, which will inspire and drive you to keep going. The more you go, the deeper the relationships become, the more powerful your work is, and the more you are driven to keep going. This creates a sustainable source of energy that drives you to continue through any obstacle you face so you can get your podcast on the airwaves.

One thing I do want to note is that while it may seem endearing to choose yourself as your "who" to represent your "why," this is un likely to be a sustainable approach. The reason behind this is that we have a tendency to be able to quickly and easily justify why we are no longer pursuing things, or why we are letting ourselves down, and we can rapidly forgive ourselves for quitting. When no one else is involved in the process, the only person you are "letting down" is yourself, and if you decide you are okay with that, then there is no real motivation to proceed. If your "who" is someone outside of yourself, though, you will be far less likely to let them down because justifying *that* becomes much more challenging. While the opportunity to let them down always exists, you will be far less likely to take that action because you know it would ultimately make you feel terrible, too.

2

DESIGNING THE PODCAST THAT
SUITS YOU

Developing a dream and defining the fuel to that dream is essential to begin any new endeavor. Unfortunately, many people stop there because they think a dream is enough, or they become overwhelmed with the idea of bringing that dream to life. You won't stop there, though. You want this way more than that.

The very fact that you clearly defined your dream and developed a specific why is evidence that you have the ability to take the necessary steps to fulfill your podcasting dreams. As you witnessed yesterday, small actions can turn into big results, rapidly. After just a few minutes, you were able to go from a vaguely defined vision and drive, to a clearly defined goal and a meaningful source of fuel to get you there. That is ultimately what the entire journey is comprised of: consistent, small steps that move you in the right direction. The more you take these small steps, the further you are moved in your desired direction, and the more success you will develop in a shorter period of time.

Today's focus is going to be on designing a podcast that suits you so that you are sure to truly enjoy podcasting and get everything you desire out of it. If, until now, you were looking into *other* people's formulas for success and trying to figure out how you might apply their approach to your success, chances are you have found a lot of contradicting information. Everywhere you look, people are providing different details on what it means to podcast, how podcasting works, how your show should be developed, and how frequently you should be sharing with your audience. The reality is, while we do have statistics that give us a general guideline as to what works, *there is no one-size-fits-all approach.* Designing a podcast that suits you ensures that you are developing a formula that fits what you can offer your podcast and what you are looking to get out of your pod cast. Remember, with podcasting you get out of it what you put into it. This means if you put nothing into it, you will get nothing out of it. Alternatively, if you put stress, over-whelm, and confusion into it, *you will get stress, over-whelm, and confusion out of it.* The real system for success is to find a way to pour passion, excitement, and joy into your podcast in a practical way that turns results, so that you can get passion, excitement, and joy out of your podcast, as well as your desired results. When you can combine a positive attitude *and* a proven method, you have a fool-proof design for success.

The three parts of designing a podcast formula that suits you and gets the results you need include: having a captivating intro, nailing the shape and size of your podcast, and having the right output frequency. The key to successfully designing these three elements is to pay attention to the statistics and use them to guide the development of your own formula so that you have something that works for you *and* provides you with the security of proven effectiveness.

Creating a Captivating Introduction

The first element of designing your own podcast is creating a captivating introduction that sells something you are able, and excited, to deliver on. Your show will actually contain two elements where you can shine here: an intro and an outro. Both can contain music, which creates a memorable show with a clearly defined identity. Your introduction, however, can go even deeper. Most podcasts have an introduction that consists of 2-5 brief sentences defining who you are, what the podcast is about, why you are making it, and what people can expect to gain from it. Explain all this in as few words as possible, so your audience does not grow bored and back out of your podcast before ever getting to the actual episode. You want to be concise, lively, and ready to jump into the episode.

Before you get into scripting your introduction, start by deciding what type of music you want to be associated with your podcast. By now, you might already have an idea of a little tune you want to use to help introduce your show. If not, that's okay; you can always take your time to think about it or browse royalty free samples of music that are available for your use. It would be best to start with a good idea as to what energy you want the music to have, or at least one aspect of sound that should be included so that you have a starting point. From there, you can start searching for soundtracks with that sound until you find the one you like. PremiumBeat.com, Ben Sound.com, and FreeMusicArchive.com are all great places for you to look if you want to get royalty free soundtracks for cheap. Once you have found one that you like, listen to it a few times to make sure it is a sound you would be interested in listening to over and over again, every time your podcast starts and ends. As well, consider how it relates to your podcast's energy, and whether or not it is something that can be easily recognized and memorized by your audience. A good podcast has consistent music in every podcast. A *great* podcast has music that can be memorized to the point where your audience hums it to themselves or gets it stuck in their head for a little while because it is so catchy. A great example of this is not actually in a podcast but is associated with the fast-food franchise known as *McDonalds*. Even if you don't eat there, you can likely sing the "Ba da ba ba ba, I'm lovin' it" jingle to yourself. Catchy jingles have been used for decades, possibly since the beginning of advertising itself. That is because these are memorable, making it easy for them to get stuck in your head so that you think about them over and over again. Even if the brand is not immediately in front of you, you might catch yourself humming the jingle and thinking about them. Thus, you are more likely to search it out and interact with it once again.

That is exactly what you want to create with your intro and outro music. The last thing you should consider about your music is whether or not you can reasonably talk over it. Podcasts are well known for their briefly descriptive introduction, and that is because this method of introducing the show *works*. You should do it for your podcast, too.

Introducing your podcast through a brief description requires you to quickly summarize your podcast in 2-5 short sentences and record it. Then, you will lay that over the introduction music and play that as your introduction for every single podcast you create. This specific introduction is not introducing the episode of the podcast, but your podcast as a whole. Introducing the specific episode can be accomplished at a later point in the development of your show.

Scripting your introduction should be as simple as saying a brief yet concise and meaningful description of your show for your followers. Since you have already put effort into defining your dream podcast yesterday, fulfilling this task should be simple! You want to quickly answer who you are, what your podcast is about, what they can expect to gain from it, and why it is worth listening to. For example, you might say, "Welcome to the Podcasting Podcast, where we dis cuss practical, actionable steps for new podcasters to achieve their big-time dreams without the confusion, hassle, or stress." This quick introduction describes who you are ("Podcasting Podcast"), what your podcast is about ("podcasting"), what they can expect to gain from it ("practical, actionable steps for new podcasters"), and why it is worth listening to ("to achieve their big-time dreams without the confusion, hassle, or stress.")

Create your introduction by scripting the answers to these four questions. Then, begin looking for ways to write them together, so they flow and create a catchy and interesting introduction. If you find you have a particularly long introduction, see if you can shorten it by getting more concise, eliminating unnecessary descriptions, or even transferring some of the introduction into the podcast episode introduction with a simple one-liner that fills in the details that your podcast introduction misses.

A few great examples of podcast introductions might include:

"Welcome to the Todd and Randy show, where we discuss everything sports related. If you're looking for a splash of entertainment mixed with some cold hard truths, you've come to the right show!"

"Welcome to the Mommy Wine show, where the focus is on wine, babies, and scratch-your-head or pee-your-pants stories of uncensored motherhood experiences."

"You're listening to the Music Podcast, where our number one focus is on the latest tracks and the brilliant minds who laid them out for us. Are you ready to be entertained?" "Ready for an hour of mystery, thrills, and downright spooky fun? Welcome to the spooky story podcast, I'm your host Jennifer, and I'm ready to slay your day."

These introductions are short, concise, and provide quick insight about your show to a new or long-time listener. Essentially, they are the perfect introductions to spark someone's interest and get excited to share time with you!

Your Podcast's Shape and Size

Designing your podcast is not just about designing an intro and outro; it is also about designing the bulk of the podcast itself. At this point, we're not talking about specific individualized episodes. Instead, we are talking about the general formula each episode will follow to ensure that it fits into the greater theme of the podcast you are creating.

The first thing you need to cover when it comes to designing your podcast is to decide what format you are going to follow. Six specific formats that, according to *Voices*, have the greatest impact on your audience. These formats will provide excellent content within each episode, as well as a cohesive flow across your entire channel. The six main formats include nonfiction narrative storytelling, hybrid, interviews or panel discussions, repurposed content, educational, and conversational. Of course, you can also blend these formats together to help you get the exact podcast you desire.

To help you understand these formats a little more, let's discuss what they are and how they work. Nonfiction narrative storytelling is a format where you actually read nonfiction stories to your listeners. These could be stories written in books, or they could be stories you come across or have submitted to you by your audience. This one is more tricky because you have to have an excellent storytelling voice that will allow you to entertain your audience, while also conveying the underlying messages of your stories.

A hybrid podcast is one that has a set podcast host, but that also frequently rotates between guests, guest hosts, and speakers who con tribute to the show so that there is plenty of diverse content from a number of different people. The difference between a hybrid and interview or panel discussion is how the show is recorded. In a hybrid, the show is rotated frequently. In an interview or panel, the host(s) always remains the same, but the people being interviewed or questioned will change from episode to episode. One can be more conversational, while the other comes off as a more traditional interview.

An interview or panel discussion format allows you to leverage others' to help you get even more content onto your show. With inter views, you might interview one person or one unified group of people (such as a band or co-owners of a small business or nonprofit group) to answer questions you have curated. For a panel discus sion, you would sit on a panel with others and answer pre-chosen questions ahead of time. In this situation, you would also be answer ing the questions, not just asking them. These are great for getting many opinions circulating, and for encouraging discussion on important topics.

Repurposed content is a format where you essentially repurpose content you have created for other mediums. For example, if you are already hosting a YouTube channel or a blog, you might use repurposed content as an opportunity to repurpose videos or blog posts. This way, rather than having to come up with brand new content, you can share the excellent content you have already created. Plus, you can start using this as an opportunity to transform your content into a format that is easy to listen on the go, or while your listeners are doing other things.

Educational podcasts are formatted to educate the audience on something over a set period of time. These range from bite-sized or short podcast episodes that provide the audience with a number of facts on a specific topic, to full-sized or longer podcast episodes that discuss certain topics in-depth. The intention is to teach the listener something new through the duration of the show. Some educational podcasts aim to provide interesting or unusual information, while others aim to educate people on something specific such as social justice or farming practices.

Conversational podcasts are formatted to include a conversational experience. The purpose here is essentially to speak into the podcast as though you were sharing a diary entry with your audience. They would then listen along to feel as though they are closer with you, while also getting a snapshot into your life. This is common among people who are developing a personal brand, or who have a life that may be particularly interesting and worth sharing about. For example, if you travel a lot, a traveling diary type podcast may be fun to share.

It is important that you choose a format that not only serves popular content, but that also fulfills your passion. You should feel as though you are genuinely connected to the content you are creating, as you want to develop a show that you will look forward to making for years to come. The more you enjoy your show, the easier it will be to make a show that everyone else enjoys, too.

After you have chosen the format for your podcast, you need to decide what the actual podcast episodes are going to look like. This means you need to decide on the length of each podcast episode, what you want to offer through that episode, and how you are going to make the episode worth listening to while also making your show worth returning for.

Deciding on the length of your podcast episodes may be tricky, as you may not feel entirely confident in what is likely to work for you. It can be easy to get caught up in defining the exact number of minutes, but the reality is that the minutes themselves are not what truly matters. What matters is what you are offering in those minutes, and whether or not they are worth listening to. If you have a show that is 60 minutes long, but the content of each episode could have been offered in as little as 20 minutes, meaning the rest of your show is really just unimportant and unexciting filler, you have a terrible podcast episode. If, however, you have a show that is 60 minutes long and full of engaging, inspiring, and exciting content that people are genuinely enjoying tuning into and that they want to keep tuning into, you have a show that is worth listening to.

One rule of thumb when it comes to podcasting is if you have a show that is going on for longer than 30 minutes, you should have at least one, if not two entertainment segments that help break up the show. Serious or deep topics that are discussed for more than 30 minutes can be dense and heavy to follow. Your audience may have a hard time consuming all of your information because you are providing it so rapidly that they start to lose focus. Breaking your show up with a small break where your audience is given a chance to mentally absorb everything you have said ensures that when you start talking again, they are more focused and actually gain immense value from your show.

Your entertainment segment could be a quiz, interesting facts, a listener engagement game, a shout out to loyal fans who have been following you for any period of time, a story submitted by a listener, a story or anecdote you heard at some point that week, or anything else. As long as you have something enjoyable that your audience looks forward to listening to, you have a great segment to help break up your show, keep it fun and interesting to listen to and keep your listeners engaged for longer.

Segments are actually an incredibly powerful tool to leverage when it comes to providing audio content on a medium such as podcast ing. With segments, you can offer plenty of high-value content in a single podcast, over specific periods of time on your show. A great example of how you could segment your show is as follows. The first ten minutes could be spent discussing current events, the next ten minutes could be about actionable steps your audience can take, and the third ten minute segment could be about inspiring your listeners. You could also include a small segment that encourages your audience to engage with you. By breaking your show up into segments, people know what to expect, they look forward to each segment, and you are able to more clearly organize your show script and experience.

Output Frequency

The last thing you need to focus on when it comes to developing your podcast is to decide how frequently you are going to upload new podcast shows. Most podcasts upload at least once per week, though others upload as often as daily or as little as once per month.

Decide on your frequency by considering your audience, your topic, and the length of each episode. If you will be uploading 15 minute episodes and you know your audience can easily digest that on a day to day basis, you might want to upload new shows daily. If, however, you will be uploading 30 minutes to hour long episodes, or longer, you will want to reduce your output frequency. Uploading fewer longer episodes means that your audience has more time to get through each episode before you upload a new one. It is also more realistic for you to create this content and sustain your output frequency.

It is important to note that despite the fact that monthly podcasts exist, they are not an ideal way to go. Monthly podcasts often have to be rather lengthy to create enough content to make up for having to wait an entire month between episodes, plus they happen so infrequently that people tend to forget about you. As well, just because you are posting monthly does not mean you can get away with a 3-4 hour episode. It would be better to break that up and deliver it weekly, rather than deliver something incredibly long once per month.

You can also determine your frequency by considering the type of content you are creating. How frequently are people interested in consuming your specific type of content? Do they want to consume it multiple times a week, once a week, or once every other week or every few weeks? The answer to these questions largely depends on what type of content you are creating. For example, if you are hosting a podcast that reviews new music, you may want to host it just once or twice per week so that you have time to listen to new music and produce thoughtful feedback on the music you have listened to. If you were hosting a podcast about the latest tech updates, though, you might want to share shorter daily episodes. This is because every day, new tech developments are being announced, and you do not want to fall behind on these trends and lose your audience to someone who is more up to date and quick about sharing.

After you have considered the average length you want your episodes to be and how frequently you will be uploading, you want to compare it to the following chart to see if you are within the right ballpark for your preferences and your audience's preferences.

The following chart compares the length of the episode to output frequency to give you an idea of what works best, and what is most realistic for you to create on an ongoing basis:

- Semi-daily episode (two per day): 1-5 minutes per episode. Daily episodes: 1-15 minutes per episode, up to 30 minutes. Weekly episodes: 15-60 minutes per episode, up to 90 minutes.

- Bi-weekly episodes: 60 minutes per episode, up to 90 minutes.
- Monthly episodes: 60-90 minutes per episode, no more.

If your chosen length and frequency are not matched up in the above chart, I highly recommend you adjust either your length or output frequency. It may seem intimidating or unmanageable right now, but you will find that with the right length and frequency, you will be able to offer plenty of high value content to your audience and frequently enough to stay relevant. If you look at this chart and feel like you have absolutely no idea what you would say or where you would begin, fear not! Starting tomorrow, we will be digging in on ways that you can maximize the quality of your show so that you have plenty of high-quality content to share, and your listeners are captivated by everything you have to say.

One last thing I must point out that it will save your sanity as a beginner is the power of batching content. Podcasters batch content as a way to streamline their time spent on each stage of producing a podcast, which results in a much less stressful podcasting experience. To batch your content, you will first determine how much time you can consecutively spend in the studio recording your podcast. Then, you will figure out how many episodes you can reasonably create in that timeframe. For example, if you have 8 hours in the studio and you are creating 15 minute daily episodes, you could reason ably create around 25 episodes in a single session. While you could technically get as many as 32, you would want to factor in time for rest, eating, bathroom breaks, and do-overs in case you make mis takes (and you will.)

During those 8 hours, you would then record all 25 podcast episodes. Next, you would edit all 25 podcast episodes at the same time. Then, you would upload them into your production suite and schedule them for their launch dates. By doing this, you streamline the process, have plenty of content made in advance, and don't have to go back and forth between recording, editing, and publishing all of your content. In the above scenario, you would only need to record for 1 day every 14 days to create enough content for a daily show.

3

UNDERSTANDING AND IMPLEMENTING THE CATALYSTS FOR AN IMMERSIVE SHOW

The design of your show should be your first focus. Once you have that down, you need to be focused on creating high-quality episodes. Your episodes need to be captivating and inspiring so your audience enjoys them and comes back for more each time you release a new one. If you are new to using the power of your voice and spoken content to create engaging con tent, it may seem strange to rely on your voice and your content to create strong relationships with your audience, while inspiring them to come back for more. Fortunately, it is much easier than you might think, and if you let yourself relax and rely on high-quality catalysts for an immersive show, you can actually have a lot of fun with this entire experience.

I find with new podcasters that their fear and tendency to hold back their voice and minimize the quality of their expression comes from not entirely understanding what gets your audience excited, or what makes them want to listen. You might also feel silly when you realize that the more expressive you are, the better, which can sometimes be the opposite of how you communicate in your day to day life. When you learn exactly what your audience needs to hear, and how they like to hear it, your audience becomes insatiable because the quality of your show explodes. This is the best way to grab the attention of your audience and keep it.

An excellent way to quickly get over the fear of sounding silly, or the discomfort that leads to you keeping your voice small, is to truly talk about something you are passionate about. Never underestimate the power of your own passion. When you are passionate about what you are talking about, you will have a hard time *not* showcasing that passion in your voice. As a result, all that expression and energy will come naturally, and you will not have to work so hard to make it happen. Plus, you will carry natural confidence with you. All of this will translate into an incredible show that people are thrilled to tune into for each new episode.

The four catalysts to developing an immersive show that will capture your listeners and bring new listeners to your show with each new episode include: using the power of your voice, writing a compelling script, building parasocial relationships, and adding explosive flavor to your podcast. The more you can incorporate these elements into your podcast, and do so with excellency, the more each episode will take off and help you truly launch into the glory podcast success.

Write Compelling Scripts

Writing scripts for your podcast is the secret sauce for making each episode as stress-free as possible. If you have already planned out what you are going to say and how you are going to say it ahead of time, there is no reason to feel pressured to figure it out on recording day. This way, on recording day, you can focus more on the power of your voice and keeping things running smoothly.

How you script your show will depend on what type of show it is. Some shows do better with a small script that keeps the host organized and focused, while other shows may be scripted all the way through to ensure the podcast is perfect from start to finish. Generally speaking, podcasts with more conversational tones or ones that are run by people who are highly confident in their recording skills are done with minimal scripting. The scripting is solely to keep the host on topic and to prevent them from spending too much time talking on any given subject. On the other hand, if you are new to podcasting or if you are talking about something that is particular, or that may require you to remember very specific information, scripting is a powerful way to help yourself along. With a proper script, you can keep yourself from having to think through what you are going to say, and instead focus solely on your delivery.

Writing your script in advance also helps reduce the amount of time you spend in the studio, as it allows you to focus solely on recording, rather than on creating content and recording it at the same time. In order to achieve this, though, and leverage the power of a script, you must write the perfect script. A proper script should follow a specific formula that allows you to cover all of the necessary content for your show, and that provides you with the ability to keep the show engaging and captivating. With the right formula, you also seamlessly flow from one point to the next, generating a cohesive and enjoyable podcast.

The general formula you should follow, per *Castos* "Podcast Script 101" is as follows:

Sponsor Message

Introduction

Musical jingle/sound effects

Longer explanation of what is in store

Topic 1
Main point
Supporting point
Supporting data
Supporting quote

Segue

Topic 2
Main point
Supporting point
Supporting data
Supporting quote

Sponsor message

Topic 3
Main point
Supporting point
Supporting data
Supporting quote

Segue

Outro

Call to action

Sponsor message

Musical jingle/sound effects

As you write your script, it is important to keep it conversational and to write it in a way that supports your delivery. Creating a conversational script ensures that your script does not come across as being too stiff or stuffy, and prevents you from developing a monotonous sound that causes people to immediately tune out. Another benefit of creating a conversational script is that it allows *you* to feel more relaxed in your delivery, and it creates more room for you to truly share your passions with your audience. Creating notes to support your delivery makes it even easier to liven up your voice and deliver a great show. This ensures you follow the proper pauses, emphasis, laughs, sighs, and other dramatic effects to brighten up your energy and make your show more enjoyable to listen to.

Even if you are brand new, you should still leave space in your script for you to go off on improvised tangents. Being able to chat on what ever comes naturally in that moment is a great way to keep the podcast more authentic and present to the moment that you are recording. Plus, this can make the recording process far more enjoyable. Remember to keep your tangents on topic so they are relevant, and don't forget that you can always edit them out at a later date if you do not particularly like them.

As you record your podcast, be mindful of descriptions and pace. Descriptions allow you to bring the listener into your experience by actually describing the experience to them in a way that draws them in. For example, if you talk about your recent trip to the grocery store, describe what grocery store you go to or offer a few descriptors to help your listener picture the scene in your mind. Don't be too extensive or in-depth, just say enough to give your audience a clear vision in their mind. As you do all of this, maintain a reason able pace, so you do not rush through the episode, or put listeners to sleep by going too slow. Speak using a conversational pace that allows you to get information across in reasonable timing, without rushing through so people miss everything you said.

Finally, be yourself. There is nothing worse than listening to a podcast, or consuming any content really, and realizing that the person is behaving as a pre-canned persona, rather than their real self. If you find yourself trying to live into a personality that does not fit you, or trying to make your personality seem more "likable," you are likely trying way too hard. While you do want to encourage yourself to have a charming and captivating persona, there is no reason to try to force yourself to be anyone other than who you are. Trust that your personality is plenty and that people will love listening to you as you are!

When your script is well-designed, it showcases your personality with excellency, and this ensures that your listeners fall in love with your content because they develop a relationship with the personality of the person sharing it... in other words, you! Being yourself and showing up in a positive impactful way is the ultimate key to gaining true fans that are willing to subscribe to your show and listen on a regular basis.

Use Your Powerful Voice

Your voice is what people are listening to. Even if they are listening for the content you are sharing; they have to receive that content through your voice. Do everything in your power to ensure you are exciting to listen to while matching the tone that best reflects your podcast's topic. You can do this by energizing yourself, smiling while you are talking, annunciating your words, and expressing yourself with great enthusiasm. Of course, be sure you do so in a way that is entirely respectful of the content you are producing. While this upbeat energy is excellent for most shows, it may not be appropriate to a show where you talk about tragedies, mysteries, or anything that might require a more serious or questioning tone. For example, if you talk about unsolved or unusual crime mysteries, you do not want to sound upbeat and cheery because that will sound completely out of place for the content. Instead, you want to sound serious, questioning, and concerned. Adjust your tone to match the content you are producing, as this allows for a much more immersive show where you've instantly captivated your listeners, delivering a podcast experience that they'll be excited to come back to. This helps your listeners to develop a deeper level of attraction to your show because of how interesting your tone makes it.

Podcast creators will often use an incredibly animated voice in their intro or outro and then will use a more muted animated voice for the bulk of their content. This is because a more animated intro immediately captures the attention of your audience and gets them curious about what you have to say. The energy you pour into your intro also transfers into your audience, getting them excited for your show and building their own energy. In this sense, it is like developing an infectious energy that your audience can't help but feel themselves. In doing so, you not only excite them for each episode but have them looking forward to listening again because they look forward to a pick-me-up during their day.

For the bulk of your episode, you do not need to speak with quite such an animated tone, but you still need to speak with energy and enthusiasm. In doing so, you continue to develop that infectious energy and support people in feeling positive while listening to you, while also encouraging them to want to listen in again for that very same reason.

Encouraging your audience to match your energy and develop excitement around your shows is not the only benefit you gain from sharing your content with enthusiasm, either. In doing so, you also create a positive association between yourself and your audience, which leads to you being able to begin to feel as though they are developing a positive relationship with you. This relationship, called a parasocial relationship, is the foundation for massive success in your role as a media producer.

Build Parasocial Relationships

As I mentioned previously, parasocial relationships are relationships that are largely one-sided, and they describe the relationships that audiences share with media figures. When you develop a podcast, whether you like it or not, you are going to be engaging in a parasocial relationship with your audience. This can be uncomfortable and even weird to get used to at first, especially if you value equal and fair treatment in relationships, as you may feel like your audience deserves more from you. The problem with this is that you cannot reasonably offer your 1:1 attention to every single person in your audience, and pressuring yourself to *have* to is a terrible idea. What will end up happening is you burn yourself out in an effort to try to maintain 1:1 relationships with your growing audience, which is never sustainable.

Rather than feeling guilty or burning yourself out, reframe parasocial relationships and understand your role within the one you share with your audience. Understanding this role will allow you to show that you value and are grateful for your audience in a way that feels meaningful for them, without draining yourself or placing unreasonable expectations on yourself.

The first way to build your parasocial relationship is to develop a persona. Your persona is a fictional representation of who you are, and the purpose of it is to create an entire "person" for people to relate with, while still giving yourself room to respect your personal privacy and life. Personas are essential in successful brands because they allow you to drive your design decisions, develop your brand, and grow your audiences without creating unhealthy demands on your personal character.

Your persona includes:

- Your host name

- Your title and major responsibilities
- A quote that defines you
- Your demographics (age, education, ethnicity, family status, etc.)
- Your goals and tasks you want to accomplish
- Your pain points or frustrations
- Your technical experience and background
- Your working environment
- Photographs of you that portray your persona
- The things you find funny, and the things you dislike Your favourite food, colour, and season
- The way you spend your time when you are not recording

As you develop your persona, I strongly encourage you to think about a persona that genuinely reflects who you are, and that can easily be promoted to your audience. Again, it all comes back to passion. You need to feel truly passionate about the persona you are creating, and you need to feel the ability to genuinely connect to your persona so you can feel deeply connected to the brand you are creating. This is key. People with personas who explode in popularity while also loving every aspect of what they do are people who have created their persona to accurately reflect who they are. This make it easier for people to believe in the persona and enjoy being around that person.

Once you have developed your persona, you need to learn how to leverage your persona and your interaction measures to create and nurture your parasocial relationships. You can do this by first understanding your role in the parasocial relationship. Your role is to be yourself, or your persona, and portray yourself in a way that allows your followers to feel personally connected with you, as they would with a friend. However, you are not giving them direct, one-on-one attention. Instead, you are offering certain aspects that allow them to know you are aware of their presence and you respect and value them, while also respecting and valuing the fact that a media persona cannot reasonably keep up with that many 1:1 relationships. It would not be healthy nor feasible.

Your role is to show up, create engaging content that people love, and continue to do so over and over again. As a result, people consume your content and "live with" you as a part of their daily lives, which creates a sense of personal connection between them and you. The bond of intimacy that is created through these relationships is an illusion, but it is a good illusion. That is, assuming that you are using it for positive purposes. As people develop this sense of connection with you, you have the power to motivate, inspire, entertain, and support them in many different ways. While it may not be 1:1, there are still plenty of valuable ways you can support people.

In order to leverage parasocial relationships to develop a powerful connection with your audience, you need to accomplish one thing over five different steps. That is, you need to accomplish the illusion of having a face-to-face experience with your audience. That is exactly why descriptive podcasts, expressive voices, and corresponding social media presences are so important. They all help build your perceived face-to-face interaction with your audience.

The first way to build your face-to-face experience is to speak directly to your audience. Use words like "you" and "us," as these words inspire a sense of belonging within your audience and encourage them to feel like they are a part of your world.

The second way to build your face-to-face experience is to share real stories. Your real stories create a sense of connection between your audience and yourself because they offer your audience the ability to resonate with you and feel a sense of emotional connection to your experience. Tell your audience's stories, too. Especially when your audience submits their own stories to you, share them, as this deepens the dynamic between you and your audience and creates an even more relatable experience for other listeners.

The third way to build your face-to-face experience is to mingle with your audience. Comment back, hang out where your audience hangs out, and become a part of the group as much as you possibly can. Even if you are not able to personally connect with everyone in these engagements, connect with as many people as you can. This way, you are a part of them, and not shouting at them from a distance. A great way to hang out where your audience hangs out, aside from offline locations, is to get into online communities where there is an active audience 24/7. Facebook groups are a great example of these audiences, as they allow you to hop on and start building relation ships with people in those groups. Make sure you engage in these groups in a way that encourages genuine engagement, and that allows you to have real, down-to-earth conversations with the members. Do not just drop a link and run, but actually participate and become a valued member of the group, as this is how you will actually capture the attention of your audience and have them interested in listening to your new podcast episodes. Now, they feel connected to you, and they want to listen to you and everything you have to say.

The fourth way to build your face-to-face experience is to create an idealized version of what your audience wants. Your audience wants something very specific in life, and you have the ability to mirror back to them that experience. For example, Liberace mirrors back the gentle and understanding husband that the audience doesn't have, or Nancy Berg shows off the idea of being the perfect housewife. You essentially want to create an image within your own life of what your audience wishes they had, and then you want to market that to them. Then, they live vicariously through you.

The fifth way to build your face-to-face experience is to become a part of everyday life. That is precisely what you are going to do with your podcast, by creating content that they can listen to while they go about their daily experiences. You will also do that by creating a social media presence that corresponds with your podcast and has people following you across multiple platforms. And, of course, you can do this by attaching your persona to a specific symbol or correlation so that whenever your audience sees that correlation, they think of you. For example, the Kardashians are heavily associated with magazines, so anytime you see magazines or similar tabloids, you will likely think about the Kardashians and wonder what they are doing. Or, at the very least, you will think about them.

Finally, I strongly encourage you to put your own spin on all of this. Do not think about it too hard, and do not make it too much of a professional choice. If you treat your persona and parasocial relationships like a business, it is going to feel extremely false for both yourself and your audience. You need to pour your passion into this and show up authentically so that it feels true to who you are and how you genuinely want to show up, as this will allow you to nurture these relationships in a meaningful way that feels good. That energy will inevitably translate into your audience and result in a back-and forth relationship that is exhilarating to uphold, and that supports you with creating everything you desire in your business, without making it feel too professional. Remember, the entire goal is to have fun! The finances are just a benefit of you having the most fun you can possibly have.

If you can create that face-to-face illusion through these five methods, you will create a persona that people immediately connect with and that they want to continue to connect with because it feels special and positive. They will relate with you, resonate with what you have to say, and genuinely begin to care about you and everything you are doing because it allows them to feel connected to someone they care about. In their eyes, they see you similar to how they would see a friend, and they care about you just the same. In your eyes, you respect and value them because they are the very reason you have the position of success you have, since your audience is what gives you the attention you need to grow your brand to successful lengths. Make sure you consider this and include it in both your show script and in your social media presence when it comes to developing your platforms and advertising your podcast to your audience.

Leverage Explosive Flavor

The one thing every successful persona is phenomenal at that others aren't taking advantage of is explosive flavor. Strong personas have a powerful capacity to infuse serious energy into everything they do, even if it is just talking into a microphone. For a podcast, that means conveying your aura through your voice, your content, and your approach. Believe me, when I say, this one thing matters *a lot* when it comes to generating success. In fact, I can virtually guarantee that you will not be successful if you do not add explosive flavor to your podcast from day one.

Your jaw-dropping personality is what turns someone into a viral sensation overnight. This is how brand new podcasters turn their shows into the most-listened podcasts in record timing, and it is how you can get yourself toward all your goals as fast as possible.

Developing an explosive flavor for your show may seem intimidating, especially if you think you have to copy someone else's flavor or do things that seem wildly unrealistic for your personality. Fortunately, that is *not* how the creation of your own signature energy and persona works. Creating the "pop" for your own personality is achieved by taking the most likable parts of your personality and turning them all the way up. If you tend to be a funny person, turn the dial up. If you are charismatic, turn the dial up. If you are charming, expressive, honest, excellent at explaining things, passionate, curious, great at asking questions, inspiring, or anything else, *turn the dial up.* Be who you are, in a loud and bold manner, and use this as your unique flavor for your explosive content.

Aside from becoming a louder version of your already awesome self, there are other practical ways you can turn the flavor up on your podcast, too. These proven methods will have your show growing rapidly and your goals being achieved with record timing.

Firstly, get incredibly clear on your persona and play into that character to the best of your ability. Always go beyond your comfort zone, and expand who your persona is so that you develop an infectious and atten-tion-grabbing personality that captures listeners' inter-est. You could also find yourself a co-host that you get along with, and who you share great chemistry with, that you can create your show with. Getting two flavorful personalities together is a great way to liven up your show even more. Plus, you will likely find that you start expanding off of each other's energy and blowing your flavor up to incredible proportions. This will make you both extremely fun to listen to.

One podcaster actually exploded his viewership on his hip hop show by having a 3 minute segment where he would freestyle rap for his audience. To create his rap, he would use comments his audience had left on his content from the previous week and turn it into a freestyle rap in that moment. This was an incredibly engaging experience that highlighted his viewers, made them feel as though they were a part of the experience, and that expanded his viewership because it was such a fun, interactive experience for the audience. While many may have come to the show to listen to his raps, the reality is that they were also growing fond of the show itself, and therefore they became devoted listeners, and it all started with a fun experience with explosive flavor.

Another great way to explode your flavor is to create a listener's spotlight. A listener's spotlight is a spot where you can promote your listener's work. This can be accomplished during the end of an episode as an opportunity to showcase your listeners and their talent, while also showing your appreciation for them. By doing this, you create a sense of back-and-forth interaction with your audience, too, in a way where you are able to give back to them. As a result, they see that there is a positive and valuable relationship being built between your listeners and you, and they are more likely to remain committed to your show, and to you.

Listener's spotlights are not the only way to create engagement, either. You can create engagement through many different methods. The more you create engagement between your listeners and your show, the better, because the more they actively listen to your show and participate in a parasocial relationship with you. One simple way to get more engagement is to ask people questions and then report their responses in your shows. For example, if you have a thriving Instagram presence where you promote your podcast, you might ask questions on Instagram and then share that question and the answers you received on your podcast. This is a great way to give your listeners a voice and allow them to partake in the development of your show.

Another great way to create engagement with your podcast would be to invite listeners to verbally share stories with you. This would work similarly to radios having callers call in and share stories, except you would have your callers send you an audio file of their story, and then you would edit it into the show. While this may seem more advanced, if you have an engaged audience and they fall with in a demographic that is fluent with technology, this can be a great way to amplify your engagement and create a fun, interactive segment of your show. If you want to go even further with this, you could invite listeners to apply to share their opinion on the show; then you could record part of the show over a platform such as zoom, or have the listener come to your recording studio if possible, and include them on your show that way. This offers your audience unique perspectives and gives your listeners a chance to chime in. At first, you will not have a large enough audience to share from or spotlight, so you will not be able to do this. A great alternative is to discuss interesting stories or highlights of general people that relate to your niche.

Simply tell the stories of people you heard about on line or through friends, and use the same "spotlight" approach. This way, as your audience grows, you can start swapping out these general stories for stories directly out of your audience, which will make for a smooth shift that grows your audience and increases viewer loyalty.

Every single episode should have something similar to all of your other episodes. Not just your intro and outro, but a segment of the show that is the exact same on every single episode. This could be a freestyle rap, a funny limerick, interesting facts, or anything else that entertains your audience and relates to your show. Try to make this segment short enough that it can be saved as an audio clip and use it to promote your show on other social media platforms. This way, your audience, and new listeners can all get a tiny sample of the new episode before it comes out, effectively building their interest and getting them excited to hear more. This is a great practice from the get go; although you might not have many listeners, getting into the habit of this off the bat will help you in the long run. In addition, you're stocked up on content that you can use for promo and now have great content for listeners who might decide to binge your content.

4

THE COMPLETE AND CONCISE GUIDE TO THE TECHNOLOGICAL SIDE OF PODCASTING

The preparation is complete, and now it is time to get into actual podcasting. This is the part where most people believe you are supposed to start, but as you now know, it is actually something that comes a little later on. Before you can get to the actual process of setting up your equipment and software and getting your podcast recorded, you need to have the right vision, fuel, plan, and show design to get you going. With all that done now, you can focus on more technical things, such as setting up your studio and preparing yourself to actually record the podcast!

If you do not come from a rich tech background, or if your background does not include audio recording, you might feel totally con fused when you start looking into all of the equipment and software that is required for you to run a podcast. With so many different pieces of equipment, types of software, and steps to be completed, it makes sense that you might get confused. I want to make sure it is incredibly simple for you to understand, and that you are able to get started with equipment that will make your show pop from the start. We can do that by covering the recording studio setup, the editing and producing setup, and the setup for getting your podcast published.

Recording

Before you begin investing in any equipment, I want to make it very clear that your focus should be on buying the highest quality equipment that is within your budget. Do not purchase the cheapest equipment you can find and wait until your podcast takes off before investing in better stuff. That is a terrible approach, as it results in you investing in low-quality equipment and then growing frustrated with trying to make that equipment work. Alternatively, do not stress your budget out and buy equipment that is far beyond what you would ever actually need for your podcast. Overspending is equally as bad, as it leads to you finding yourself out a lot of money in exchange for something that you could have accomplished for much less. Find a happy medium by creating a reasonable budget and affording the best quality equipment within your budget.

The equipment you will need includes: a microphone, headphones, and a quiet place for you to record your content.

Never rely on the microphone built-in to your computer, cellphone, or headphones. These microphones will not give you clear audio that is free of interference, and it will not convert well onto higher quality speakers. A great microphone for any starter, which will serve professional-level sound quality at an affordable price, is a Blue Yeti USB Mic. It plugs directly into your computer, and is a condenser microphone as opposed to the standard dynamic type. Another great condenser mic to look into would be the Rode NT1A or NT2A, both of which are excellent for recording with. However, to use non USB condensers like such, you would need a mixer or audio interface to connect these devices to your computer, which can make this route more expensive.

It is not recommended that you get a dynamic microphone, as they are just simply not as suited to podcasting as a condenser - the reason being, to put it simply, that condenser microphones are more sensitive in picking up sounds, so they are better quality for recording things that either aren't too loud or have more intricate sounds through a variety of frequencies - both of which apply to the human voice. Since the listening experience is the entire purpose of a podcast show, it is important that you focus on buying an excellent quality mic to create that high quality listening experience right from the start. The investment will be well-worth it in the long run.

Regardless of what type of microphone you invest in, it is important that you get a pop shield. Pop shields go over your microphone or sit in front of your mic and prevent it from picking up the plosives on p's and b's, which both give sudden bursts of high pressure into the mic as you are speaking. The pop shield is incredibly inexpensive and will improve your sound quality exponentially. If you can not purchase one, consider making one by taking a wire coat hanger and pulling it apart, so it creates an "O" shape, then covering it with nylons. You can then set that about an inch or two in front of your mic, keeping it close enough that it works, but far enough away that it does not touch your mic and destroy your sound quality.

When you are recording, headphones are important as they will allow you to clearly hear your recordings and create higher quality recordings right away. It is important to get over the ear headphones, and not just earphones, as these will give the best surround sound and will allow you to immediately pick up on any sound errors or strange background noises that may be interrupting your recording. A pair of Audio-Technica ATH-M30X would be great, as they are inexpensive and provide excellent sound quality. Another benefit of over-the-ear sound blocking headphones is that you can wear them while you are recording, which allows you to drown out any background noises. The less you hear yourself, and the more you can focus on recording, the better quality your show will be. Not wearing your head-phones and listening to yourself can become very distracting and may cause you to become self-conscious, minimize your expressions, or otherwise reduce your overall recording quality due to distractions or excessive self-analyzing. Leave that part for later when you are editing.

The final element of recording is to have a proper recording space. Your recording space should be sound-proof, relatively small, so your voice does not echo, and where you will not be interrupted. If you have to record at home, consider using a walk-in closet, or even a smaller room in your home such as a smaller home office or a bed room. If external noise is a concern, consider lining the walls with egg cartons or cardboard, or surrounding yourself with heavy-duty curtains to keep external noises out. If you do not have access to that, consider going to the middle of a field in a large park where you are unlikely to be interrupted by people or traffic and record there, on a day when there is no wind.

Once everything is set up and ready to record, you will only require one piece of software to get you recording. That is, a piece of software that allows you to record and store your audio locally to your device. Skype is an excel-lent tool, as you can record yourself talking and store it, or you can record a conversation with a guest you may have on your show and store that. I recommend Skype for this because it is inexpensive, works in the most straightforward manner, and allows you to store your sound locally. If you want something a little more advanced, try Ringr, which is anywhere between $8-19/month and offers excellent recording abilities, too. I like Ringr because it is made specifically for podcasters, which means you get high-quality sound, a straightforward platform, and excellent storage options so you can store any audio you record over the platform. Your guests can download Ringr, too, which allows them to call in to your Ringr account and gain access to all of the same great benefits, meaning it is also wonderfully easy for your guests to take advantage of, too.

It is important to keep things as simple as possible, especially early on, as you will already have a lot of things that are fairly new to you at this point, and complicating any step of the process will only make your podcast a challenge. Instead, keep it simple, focus on producing high-quality content with what you have, and worry about advancing different parts of the process later on.

The Editing and Production Setup

Your editing and production setup relies more on software, which is used to improve your sound quality, add in your intro and outro, and edit out any parts which you do not want to be presented on your episode. If you have an Apple computer, you will already have Garageband installed. This is an excellent platform for editing audio on. If you are using a PC, look into Adobe Audition, Audacity, or Reaper. These are all free platforms you can use to edit audio that will provide you with excellent tools at no expense. If you want something more advanced, Logic Pro is a great platform that offers semi-professional features, though it will require an investment on your behalf since it costs around $250 in the United States. For either Mac or Windows I would also recommend Avid Protools, which is the industry standard for Music and Film Production is the most powerful software available and ranges from £250 all the way up to £2500.

While editing your podcast can help you polish it up, it is important to understand that you should not be aiming to spend hours in the editing process. Instead, you should be investing in high-quality equipment so that your recordings are already high quality from the start. The editing process should be a quick, simple process where you polish the sound, add your intro and outro, include any sound effects that you may want to use, and cut out any clips of audio that you do not want in the final rendering of your episode.

You can simplify your editing process by following these exact steps:

1. Apply a fade to the beginning and end of any audio clips in your project, as this provides a smoother transition from clip to clip. If you have just one audio file, you will only need to do it at the beginning and end. If you have clipped out parts or placed multiple files together, though, you will need to apply fades to the beginning and end of every single file. If you add sound effects, you will add fades to the beginning and ending of those, too.

2. Render your audio through a high-pass filter. High pass filters eliminate unwanted low frequencies from your audio so that it does not have a "muddy" or "boomy" sound to it. All high frequencies will pass through the filter, but everything else will be eliminated, giving you a much higher quality finished sound piece. Set your filter between 80-100 Hz, as this ensures nothing lower gets through. The human range is 20 to 20,000 Hz, and the average human voice range is 85 to 180 Hz for a male or 165 – 255 Hz for a female. Setting your filter around 80-100 or even a little higher if you are a female ensures

that nothing aside from your voice gets through to the final rendering of your audio.

3. Compress your audio file so that you do not have such a dynamic range of audio in your final rendering. Compressing your file ensures that no matter what type of speaker your audience is listening through, they can hear you properly. Not doing this can result in certain parts of your audio being cut off or difficult for your listener to hear, depending on what type of speaker they are listening on.

4. Export your audio using the bounce feature so that your final audio file is stored locally to your computer and able to be uploaded to your website, social media, or any platform where you might be hosting your podcast.

I must repeat one more time that it is essential that you get a high quality recording first, then edit your already-high-quality file. You cannot edit quality into a podcast recording; you can only improve existing quality. Attempting to perfect a low-quality piece of audio will result in you still having a low-quality piece of audio in the end, even if you have begun to see some improvements with your audio.

It is also important to take some time to get acquainted with your editing software so that you are able to use it effectively with your sound files. These days, most software is quite intuitive, meaning they are capable of providing high-quality sound with little effort. As well, the interfaces are extremely user-friendly and can help you develop excellent sound without all of the confusion or a need for extensive technical experience. If you do find yourself struggling, YouTube offers great videos on how to use most software so that you can figure out how to work your software properly and achieve excellent results.

Getting Your Podcast Published

The last setup you need to know about is the part where you get yourself published. You can either publish yourself to social media, to your website, or to a platform that airs podcasts on platforms such as Apple's Podcast app.

YouTube can be an excellent spot to upload your podcast, as it supports audio and is able to be embedded on most other platforms. Since this is a video-based platform, you will want to either record video at the same time or create some sort of visual for your audience to look at. While YouTube is a great starting platform, I do recommend moving to a better audio platform as soon as possible so you can host your podcast on platforms like Apple Podcasts, Spotify, iHeartRadio, or TuneIn.

If you want to upload your Podcast to your website, turn it into an MP3 or WAV file and upload it directly to your self-hosted website. Many podcasters will do this by creating a blog page and then up loading files into individual blog posts with a short description of what that day's episode was about and what they can expect to find. This is also an excellent option if you plan on marketing products for sponsors in your videos because you can share links to those products in the blog post so listeners can easily grab those links at the end of the show.

SoundCloud, Blubrry, BuzzSprout, Anchor, and Podbean are also great platforms that you can share your podcast on. These platforms will allow you to share directly on an audio based site, and you can direct your listeners over to your profile on that platform so they can find and listen to you. If you want to get your podcast on iTunes, Spotify, or any other similar provider, you will need to create an account with that provider, submit your podcast for approval, and then wait for it to happen. Once it is approved, it will go live, and you will have your show hosted natively within these apps. Doing this is worthwhile if you want your podcast to be easily accessible, as these larger platforms are already massively popular among the podcast listening community, which means that they will be far more likely to find you and listen to your content.

5

THE 4TH DIMENSION: GUESTS, RESEARCH, AND ESSENTIAL INTERVIEW SKILLS

T he 4th dimension of hosting your podcast includes having guests on your show, or bringing others into the creation process. Many beginners will skip over the 4th dimension, as they want to create their shows for themselves, which is perfectly fine. You can absolutely run a show entirely solo and have an excellent turnout. However, adding guests from time to time, or even on a regular basis, can help your show experience rapid growth, while also providing even more value to your listeners. Plus, hosting guests can be incredibly fun as you get to engage in real, back-and forth discussion with others who are passionate about the same topics as you are, and then hear the feedback from your audience as they listen to the episode.

To create a high quality 4th dimension for your show, you need to expand your ability to research and interview others so you can create a high quality episode with your guest. Knowing how to ask the right questions, drive the show in a positive direction, and create a clear outcome for your audience is an important part of bringing guests onto your show.

Even if you are 100% new to hosting any form of online content, you can be an incredible host and interviewer right from the start. All it takes is some knowledge, practice, and a willingness to do your best from the start.

Attracting and Hosting Guests on Your Show

Step one: delete the idea that beginners cannot attract and host guests on their show right now. Just because you have a brand new show or a show that has not even been released yet, does not mean that people are not interested in being guests on your show. Although you may be doubting yourself or feeling inferior based on your lack of completed episodes to serve as proof, *many* people are going to understand your vision, believe in you, and get excited about collaborating with you. Even if no one knows who you are, this will be true. The key is to get yourself into groups where people want to have a chance to speak about what they are passionate about, and who are speaking about content that is relevant to your podcast, and then put the offer out there. *They. Will. Come.* You can be confident in that.

The more you host guests and provide excellent shows, the more guests will come around, and the more opportunities you will have to host more guests. I strongly advise that even if you intend on hosting a solo show, you create a segment or special episodes devoted to hosting guests. Guests offer an exciting, new, and unique perspective for your audience, and if they have their own audience they may bring even more viewers to your show. While they may come for the episode that your guest is in, they will stay when they realize how enjoyable your show is.

Your guest can be anyone from a friend to someone in your industry who can offer content for your audience. Early on, you may feel more comfortable interviewing friends or people that you already know as this helps you feel more confident talking with them, which can create a more enjoyable show to listen to. Even if you do not have any friends to host, though, you can still create excellent chemistry with any guest by being willing to talk to them like they are a friend. You can also develop that chemistry by researching your guests before the interview, which we will talk about in a moment.

Once you have a show on the go, you can also intentionally market your desire to host guests on your show. Include a quick blurb at the end of your show, write about it on social media platforms, and let your audience know the opportunity to be a guest is available. This encourages them to reach out to you so they can apply for a guest opportunity, rather than you always having to reach out to potential guests. This way, you have a steady instream of guests who are ready to share and bring their audience with them.

~

Guest Preparation That Guarantees a Smooth Sailing Interview

Researching your guests before the interview, even if you are already familiar with them, is a great way to get yourself prepared for the interview. As you research your guests, you give yourself the opportunity to develop a greater sense of charisma between yourself and their persona before the show. The show also becomes more enjoyable to record because you are not spending time on superficial conversation but instead connecting on a deeper level right from the start. Now, rather than asking the basics, you can invite them to maybe state a summary for your audience, and then you can dig into the juicy details.

Having the capability of getting your interviews into juicy details means that you will create both an exciting show to record and an exciting show to listen to. For you,

you will feel a natural sense of energy, charisma, and excitement washing through yourself and your guest as you both dig deeper into your passions and share in them through a lively conversation. This means that while the process of recording your show may be more of a fun appointment with a friend, and a great learning opportunity, rather than a strictly business type meeting.

For your audience, they will naturally pick up on that energy of you going deeper with your guest and sharing that passion with each other. As they listen, they will feel the excitement and synchronicity flowing between yourself and your guest, which creates a feeling as though they are right there with you, listening to that conversation live. This breaks down the wall between your audience and yourself, making it feel like they are having a live experience and deepening the connection between them and yourself.

To develop this lively energy through research first, there are three steps you are going to take. First, you are going to get a general sense of who your guest is so that you understand what they have to offer your show. Next, you are going to decide on your angle of focus and research them in a way that allows you to really narrow in on a topic and energy that will serve your show. Then, you are going to finalize your questions and arrange them in a way that draws the energy of the show into deeper and deeper levels of passion as you go.

Ideally, you should have a general sense of who your guest is *before* you invite them on the show. Not knowing who they are or what they have to offer can lead to you bringing on a guest that may be rather boring for you to interview, or it may result in you having an interview that barely, if at all, gets into a positive synchronicity. If you are approaching people to invite them to be on your show, make sure you take the time to research them first so that you know if they will be a good fit. First, research their industry and niche of knowledge to ensure they know what you will be talking about and that they will have plenty to bring to the table. Then, consider their personality. Do they have a personality that you mesh well with? Will you have fun interviewing this person? Does it seem like you would be able to get plenty out of an interview with them? If you were to spend one hour on a call together, would it be enjoyable, or do you think you would have to pull the conversation along and really push to get that show where you wanted it to go? Always consider the fun factor because if that chemistry does not exist between you and a guest member, it will make the process of recording your show extremely boring, and possibly even frustrating. You might also have a hard time standing behind the content you have created because it does not reflect your usual energy and passion. Make sure every possible guest is qualified, passionate, and that you share chemistry *before* you bring them on the show.

Some of the questions you should ask yourself as you research your guest include:

- Who are they, where are they from, what is their story? What is their personality like?
- How can you structure the interview to draw out the best of their personality, making the show more enjoyable for your audience?
- How or why are they relevant to your niche?
- Why will your audience be interested in listening to them?
- What specific topic do you want to discuss with them? Why? How are they able to contribute to this topic?
- What can they teach your audience? Why are they qualified to teach this?

If you open a forum for people to apply, this is the best way to ensure that you are getting qualified people who are eager to be a part of what you are doing. This also puts you in a unique position where you can ask for their bios and conduct small interviews with them to see how your shared chemistry feels. Since you are inviting people for interviews and not promising positions right away, you can use this as an opportunity to be a bit picky and only host guests who are truly a great pairing with your show. Again, look for passion, chemistry, excitement, and a fun time talking about topics that are highly relevant to your audience.

After you have researched the general bio of a person, you need to get more specific and decide on the topic for your show, and the angle you will take when interviewing someone. Chances are if you have picked a great guest, the two of you could happily go on for *hours* talking about your passions. The problem is, podcast episodes are finite in length, and while you can certainly host a two or three part series with one guest, you do not want to go overboard and take away from the purpose of your show. This means you need to go into the interview with a clear focus and understand how that focus is going to deepen the passion and excitement in the interview itself.

Let's say you run a podcast about personal development for entrepreneurs, for example. You could talk to anyone about any personal development topic for hours, however you only have a set amount of time to talk about something in your episode. You need to find a specific topic that your guest can passionately discuss and discover how that particular topic will fit in with your show. By choosing this one aspect, you give the show a focus, have the opportunity to build the episode up as something educational and complete for your audience, and gain the opportunity to let your guest really dig into what they are experts at. Knowing how to do this ensures that your episode really digs into juicy details, rather than floating around on a surface level.

If you can provide that deep level of knowledge to them through each episode, you will keep your listeners focused. It may feel uncomfortable or like you are alienating certain listeners from time to time to be so specific in your episodes, but remember that they are all flowing together as a part of a bigger picture. Your audience would rather have fewer exceptional quality episodes they can relate to, rather than many that are not detailed enough to be worth listening to.

Finally, you need to finalize your questions. When you are conducting an interview, many questions will occur naturally in the conversation, and you should let them. The more authentic the conversation is, the easier it will flow, and the more you will enjoy recording interviews. Aside from authentic conversational questions, ask specific questions that keep the interview rolling, too. These specific questions should be developed in a way that allows you to direct the interview so you stay on topic so you can teach your audience something specific, while deepening the discussion, and while giving plenty of room for authentic conversation to take place.

Your average interview should have one structured question for every five minutes, as this allows plenty of time for authentic discussion to happen around the answers. Of course, you may need to adjust this if you have limited time to conduct an interview, such as if your shows are 20 minutes or less. In this case, you may want to arrange for one question every 3 minutes, which would give you more questions to answer, making the interview more efficient.

The questions should be broken down into three groups. The first group will happen over the first 2-5 questions, depending on the length of the interview, and they should invite your guest to offer some form of back story or information about themselves. Remember that your audience will already know you are a credible source, but your guest will need a few minutes to build up rapport and establish credibility. Answering these questions gives them a chance to do so while also introducing them to your audience.

The bulk of your questions, which should make up around half of the total questions, should be about digging into their knowledge base or essentially picking their brain. You want to ask as many questions about their unique field of knowledge as you can, as this allows you to deepen the conversation and extract great levels of information for yourself and your audience. For example, if you were hosting a parenting podcast, you might ask a stay at home mom about how she structures her day, decides on activities to do, and overcomes daily challenges. This method of specific and deep questioning would apply to any topic you may be talking about. You want to get into the meat of the topic by digging deep, asking questions, and stringing them in a cohesive way so that it makes sense when you move from one question to the next.

The final group of questions you ask should be an inviting summary, while also encouraging your guest to leave your audience with a lesson of sorts. This is their opportunity to give your audience 1-3 take away points that they can apply to their everyday life starting right away so that they can begin to see results in their own lives based on whichever topic you have been discussing. It is important that your audience is always left with some form of action steps, as this allows them to feel like they have actually gotten something out of the interview, and they can start to see the results from those action steps. As a result, they are more likely to come back and listen to even more episodes, because they realize that your podcast is not only a blast to listen to, but it actually helps them get more out of their lives, too, either by teaching them something, or by providing them with a wonderful means of entertainment.

Creating a Conversational Interview Style That Flows

Creating a conversational interview style that flows is not just about creating a podcast that is easier for your audience to listen to; it is also about creating a podcast that you actually enjoy recording. There is nothing enjoyable about finding yourself sitting in a booth feeling trapped in a requirement to talk in an overly stuffy manner, as though you were interviewing people for a medical study. In fact, if you are not careful, a stuffy interview style could lead to you *resenting* your podcast because it makes it so unenjoyable, and could lead to you feeling like there is no way you can keep going. Since this is all about developing your passion, it is important that you never create this sort of resentment for yourself within your show design.

Creating a conversational interview style starts with proper research and preparation for your show, which you have already completed. Now, you need to make sure your chosen questions nurture conversation, and that you actually ask them in a way that encourages it, too. This will start to come more naturally as you continue practicing, so be patient with yourself and give yourself a chance to relax into the experience and go with the flow. The more you settle into the conversation, the easier it will be to have an actual conversation al type interview.

Some great conversational type questions you might ask include:

- Tell me about the overall journey that got you into this passion, what did that look like?
- Who are your biggest role models in this industry?

- What gets you really excited about the work you are doing?
- What are some of the biggest mistakes you made while learning what you have learned so far?
- If you could do anything to make this industry even better, what would you do?

These types of questions are open-ended, invite for a conversation to form, and leave for many secondary questions to be spontaneously included as that authentic conversation develops. For example, if your guest responds to who their biggest role models are, you might ask them why those are their role models, or when they started looking up to those individuals as role models. These are great ways to really expand on the interview and make it feel like a positive back and-forth experience while learning more about your guest and having a great deal of fun.

Another way to make it conversational is to keep your eye on the clock to make sure you ask your next questions on time but to not make it feel rushed. About one minute before you need to ask the next question, let your guest wrap up what they are saying and then respond with something in a short summary of what you have just discussed. Then, lead into your next question. If you have organized your questions properly, they should naturally flow one into the next. If you do end up going in a totally different direction, make sure you highlight that fact in the conversation. This way, your guest and audience know that you are changing topics and do not get confused by the switch. This makes your show easier for people to follow and makes it feel like you are still enjoying a conversational experience.

If you are going to do conversational interviews on your show, strive to make sure that the episodes are long enough to allow for plenty of enriching discussion. While you can definitely fit 15 minute interview segments into a larger show, that may not always be enough if you want to dig deep into a certain discussion. If you prefer shorter interview segments like this, consider having special episodes every so often, which is a full-episode interview. This makes these episodes extra special, as they are different from your usual pace and offer a lot of valuable content to your audience. This is a great way to mix it up and give plenty of added value, without entirely straying away from a structured show with different segments, if that is the design you prefer.

Lastly, make sure you listen to your interviews after you conduct them and look for opportunities to relax and conduct more fluid and conversational interviews. However, do not listen to them immediately after you record them or you might find yourself judging yourself too harshly, which can lead to you actually feeling even more self-conscious in your next interview, and growing more uncomfortable with your interviewing style.

Instead, give yourself a day or so, then listen to the interview with the desire to look for opportunities to improve. Choose 1-2 things you can improve on after each interview, and make a point to improve on those things the next time you are interviewing someone. This way, your interviews improve over time, and you are able to feel more comfortable and confident along the way. You will find you enjoy interviews far more if you take this approach, as you are making it more about having fun and enjoying yourself than anything else, and that will shine both in your experience and the final episode that you put out for your listeners to enjoy.

6

LAUNCHING MADE SIMPLE

Getting your podcast ready to put out there is an exciting time, and then comes the launch. In the digital world, launching is often talked about as being a stressful and overwhelming time that can leave you feeling like a mess afterward. While inefficient launch strategies can certainly make you feel like you have bitten off way more than you can chew, launching does *not* have to be that challenging. Launching can be as effortless as you make it, and, in fact, it should be effortless. The idea is that your launch, and any marketing you ever do, should always be an extension of your passion and a part of the fun of running your podcast. Yes, at times, you are likely going to find yourself feeling somewhat stressed out or overwhelmed by the different operations of your podcast. However, the majority of your experience should be fun, and that includes launching.

Before you get into any specific details about launching, resolve to choose a strategy that suits your personality and your persona, and that matches the energy of your podcast. You must do this before you do anything else because everything that comes next will be built on this foundation. If you fail to do this first, you will find your branding and marketing strategies do not fit your podcast accurately, and the whole thing feels "off." The more personalized this experience is to you and your podcast, the more joy you will have in it, and the more attention you will attract to your podcast through your energy. You read that right: *joy sells.* Joy is the number one ingredient of getting people to pay attention, and the more you enjoy what you are doing, the more success you will have.

Everything You Need to Know About Distribution and Hosting

Let's get the stressful parts out of the way, first. Distribution and hosting may seem stressful because there are so many different platforms out there. It is likely that you want to get your podcast on all the major platforms, as this is where you are likely to reach the widest viewership. The easiest way to get your distribution and hosting system set up is to break it down into independent steps and go from there.

The first step is to create your podcast. Develop your intro and outro, record your show, and get the audio ready so that your podcast can be uploaded to a system.

Step two is to turn to your primary host. You *need* a primary host, as this host is going to make it easy for you to upload your podcast to every single platform. They are essentially designed for the distribution process. If you do not already have one, Libsyn, Buzzsprout, and Podbean are all great platforms you can use to get your content in front of your audience. When you have your host chosen, you will register your new show and set up the information regarding your show into your host. Each platform will have you do this slightly differently, but the general idea will always be that you upload the name of your show, the show description, the web address and slug for your show, and other information regarding the type of show you are producing. Some of this information is going to include information that is relevant to major distribution sites, such as iTunes. It is recommended that you input this information, as this will allow your host to interact with the distribution channel, effectively making your show easier for viewers to find.

Once you have set up your host, you need to find your main feed or your RSS feed. Your RSS feed is important, as it contains the link you will require when it comes to sharing your podcast with distribution platforms. The link of your primary podcast, such as your personal website link, is *not* the link the directories will be looking for. They want the RSS feed link for the show you are hosting, as this is how they validate it and allow your podcast to be hosted on their platform.

Step three is to upload your mp3 media file for your podcast. This is where you are going to upload the final version of your podcast episode to the platform. Once everything is set up, you will skip step two and jump straight to step three as you upload your shows to your host, because everything else will already be set up for you.

Step four is to let all of the directories, such as iTunes, know that your show exists. It is important that you get your show on iTunes right away, even if you only have one episode so far because this ensures that your connection is working. Even if you load everything up to iTunes right away, you do not have to do an official launch yet. You can use this as an opportunity to adjust everything and get it ready. Meanwhile, you can continue promoting your podcast for launch.

In order to get your podcast up on iTunes in particular, you need to go to iTunes and set up an account with them. Then, you need to go to podcastsconnect.apple.com so you can set up a new show. There, you will include your RSS feed by adding the URL for your RSS feed. Remember, this is not your personal website feed, but the RSS feed from your podcast hosting website.

After you submit it, you will hit "validate," and Apple will validate your podcast. This should only take a few minutes. You will immediately see a display of your podcast on the screen, where it will show your podcast's image and all of the information regarding your podcast such as the title, language, and description. If there are any errors, these will be displayed as well so that you can fix those errors. As soon as you have, you can validate the RSS URL again, and then Apple should say "submit" so you can actually submit the show for distribution. At that point, your show with all of your current episodes will be available for live viewing on iTunes.

The same general process works for Stitcher and Google Play, as well. For Stitcher, you will go to the Stitcher website, create an ac count, and then go to Stitcher.com/content-providers, which will allow you to follow the exact same process to get your podcast live on Stitcher. For Google Play, you will create an account and then go to G.co/podcastportal to get your Podcast live on that platform, too. It is important that you get your podcast live on all three, as these are the major podcasting websites where you are most likely to get found. As well, this makes your podcast easily accessible to your audience as they can enjoy your content on apps they already have downloaded on their smart devices.

After everything has been set up the first time around, the hardest part is over. The only thing to do now is to upload future shows to your host site so they can go live.

All of your newly uploaded episodes should become available within an hour of them being uploaded to your hosting account.

The Most Effective Launch Strategies (Grand Opening VS. Soft Opening)

Once you have your podcast properly linked to your host and distribution channels, you need to start thinking about your actual launch strategy. Your launch strategy does not just define your process of getting your podcast out there, but your process of actually marketing your podcast to an audience so that people know where to find you.

There are two different types of launch strategies when it comes to getting your podcast out there: a grand opening and a soft opening. A grand opening is a wonderful way to drive a lot of attention to your podcast from day one and to help get your viewership up right away. A soft opening is excellent if you want to get started and then build attention later, when your podcast already has some episodes up and ready to go. There are pros and cons to each launch method; you will need to decide what is accurate for you and your launch.

A grand opening is wonderful because it gets a lot of attention on your podcast right away. However, if you tend to be shyer, or if you are worried about people not necessarily liking your podcast, it may make you feel intimidated by your own launch as you realize suddenly you have a lot of eyes on your content. Grand openings are a great way to generate a lot of traffic from day one, so it is important that you are ready to impress that traffic and give them a reason to stick around from day one, too.

Soft openings are wonderful because they help you develop a greater sense of confidence in podcasting, while growing your personal style. They do, however, result in minimal attention on your podcast from the start, which can make it more challenging to grow your podcast over time. Despite this, a soft opening can be excellent if you are just getting into podcasting as a hobby or for fun, and it can help decrease the pressure from you as you do not have to worry about a consistent uploading schedule or marketing. At first, you might find yourself struggling for a while to get algorithms to realize that your podcast is sought after and worth listening to. Once you get the momentum rolling, though, it should be excellent for getting your content out there.

If you want to follow a grand opening strategy, the most important thing you can do is create a presence for your podcast and start driving as much traffic there as possible, before your podcast even launches. Your presence for your podcast should consist of pages on major social media platforms, such as Facebook, Instagram, or Twitter. You can also have a self-hosted website where you create a land ing page and invite people to opt-in to a newsletter so you can email them updates about your podcast, including about the launch itself. Once your presence is set up, post about your upcoming podcast, let your friends and family know and invite everyone to share the news about your new podcast with everyone they know. You can also run advertisements to generate more attention, as this will get more traffic to your pages. The idea here is to get as many people excited about your podcast as possible so that when you do launch it, you have a major audience to launch it to. Through this, you should get a lot of traction from day one, and your primary focus will be to keep that engagement going as you continue to launch new episodes.

If you prefer to do a soft launch, you should still create a presence for your podcast, but you do not necessarily want to promote your presence. Rather than doing everything in your power to drive traffic there and get everyone excited for your podcast, your focus should be on just putting out podcasts and getting a small circle of people listening to it. For example, your friends and family and any recommendations you may get along the way. Once you get comfortable with the entire process of hosting a podcast and launching episodes, then you can start ramping up your advertising, so get yourself even more traction. At this point, you would want to start looking at advertisements and getting yourself out there as much as possible.

It is important to understand that the grand opening is always the best idea for your podcast, as it will give you the best opportunity to get yourself out there and let your passions be seen and heard by the world. If, however, you find that you do not have the experience, you are not yet comfortable with a huge audience, or you do not have the budget to support advertisements and such, you can always start with a soft launch first. As soon as you feel comfortable advertising in a bigger way, that should become your primary focus.

Regardless of what I, or anyone else, says is the best route, *do what is right for you.* Let this podcast be as enjoyable as it can be. If that means making a big bang and jumping into the podcast scene with lots of excitement, do that. If it means taking the soft opening approach and giving yourself time to warm up or save up a greater budget to get yourself out there, do that instead. There is no right or wrong answer here, as long as you are putting the energy into getting yourself out there and growing your audience.

The 7 Do's and Don'ts of Launching Your New Podcast

To make launching as easy as possible, I have comprised a quick list of 7 do's and don'ts you should know about before you get into the launch process. These rules apply whether you are launching a new show or new episodes. When it comes to promotion in any format, it is important that you always adhere to strict guidelines to avoid promoting in a way that comes across as tacky, or that drives your audience away. Tasteful promotion is actually simpler than any other strategy and will get you the best results every single time.

DO Leverage Your Existing Communities

First and foremost, always leverage your existing communities. If you are already in Facebook groups, hanging out on forums, or even partaking in offline communities, leverage them. Talk about content related to your podcast, be an active member of these communities, and build strong relationships with the people you meet in them. Make your number one point to be about engagement, not about talking about your page, as engagement is what will get you the best results. Show up as a human and a friend first, and then use the interest people have in you as an opportunity to share your podcast with them. This is an excellent way to get to your first 100 listeners.

DO Add Valuable on-Topic Content to These Communities

When you are partaking in these communities, make sure everything you do is on-topic. Avoid coming into any community and trying to "take over" or sharing about things that are entirely irrelevant, as this will lead to two highly unwanted experiences. First and foremost, you will not be talking to your target audience in a way that captures their attention and gets them excited about your show, which means your energy will be wasted. Second, it makes you look tacky because it makes it seem like you cannot participate in a group and stay on topic, so they no longer want to be a part of your audience. Always join groups that are on-topic and relevant to your niche, and then stay on-topic in those groups. That is the fastest way to grow your audience in a tasteful, attraction-marketing based manner.

DO Join MULTIPLE Facebook Groups That Are Relevant to Your Niche

Never limit yourself to just one or two spaces. Always join multiple groups that are relevant to your niche, and if you can join them as your podcast's business page, rather than your personal page. Make a point to participate in all of them. If you can, set aside several 15-30 minute blocks of time every single week and then get into those groups and start participating. Even just a few minutes in each group, commenting, posting engaging content, and sharing your knowledge with people is a great way to build those relationships and get yourself out there. The more you engage, the more people will want to know about you and will pay attention to your podcast, too. Another platform to look into outside of Facebook would be Reddit or Tumblr, both full of threads with people seeking information that is exactly what you have been sharing on your podcast.

Whenever you join a social media group to share about your podcast, there is one golden rule you MUST follow. That is: do *not* spam the community with your content. Posting too much content about yourself and your podcast, dropping links and ignoring the rest of the group, or generally failing to participate except to talk about yourself and your podcast is a terrible way to get attention on your podcast. You must participate in these groups, build up relationships and rapport, then share your content if you want to generate success with this marketing approach. Otherwise, people will think that you are too spammy, and therefore your show is likely also spammy or low-quality and will not want to listen to it, no matter how good it may actually be.

DO Learn How To Leverage SEO

SEO, or search engine optimization, is a necessary tool to understand if you want to get your podcast out into the world and develop a massive following. Everything from Google to Facebook and even Reddit uses a search engine algorithm to help decide what types of content to show to their audience, and you need to know how to leverage that algorithm to get views. There are three key steps when it comes to content SEO, regardless of where you are posting that content. The three steps include: relevancy, keywords, and quality.

Your audience is already looking content up and inter-acting with specific types of content online. Algorithms recognize this and show content that is relevant to these specific topics or search terms, so having relevant content ensures that you show up within your audience's feed or search results.

Keywords are specific words that your audience is looking up or using. Algorithms find these keywords either based on the fact that they were specifically searched, or based on the fact that the posts your audi-ence is paying attention to all share these words in common. Having these keywords in your post, in moder-ation, ensures that search engines see you as being rele-vant and show your content in their posts. This is different from overall relevance because here you are targeting specific words, while with relevancy you are targeting a specific overall topic.

Lastly, the quality of your content matters because search engines and other algorithm-based platforms do not want to be showing low-quality content to their viewers. Using language that is easy to read, written in a correct manner, and that offers value to your audience ensures that your content is high quality so algorithms will be more likely to show it.

DO Upload 3 Episodes on Day One

On the first day, you launch your podcast, regardless of whether you do a grand opening or a soft opening, you need to upload 3 podcasts. 3 podcasts give your listener a variety of content to listen to so that they can choose their favorite episode and then binge watch the rest. Although modern people have a shorter attention span than ever before, if they do find themselves thoroughly enjoying something, they will want to consume as much content from said thing as possible. Having episodes for them to choose from, and additional episodes for them to listen to right after, gives them the opportunity to fall in love with your content enough to binge on it.

Having new listeners binge on your content is actually important to your SEO, too. The steps you took previously with relevancy, keywords, and quality were all done in an effort to get people to consume your content. The more they consume your content, the more algorithms will assume they enjoy your content and will show you in their feed. This means you will show up consistently throughout their feed, rather than just every so often, which means you will get more engagement. As your engagement goes up, so will your reach and therefore your following will grow, too.

DON'T Follow a Weak Uploading Schedule

In your first weeks after launching a podcast, you should be uploading at least three shows per week. Even if you intend on uploading fewer than that in the future, three per week is an important place to start as it allows you to accumulate plenty of great content, and fast. This means that your existing audience has plenty of content to listen to, and any newcomers who stumble upon you have plenty of great content to binge on. The more you upload, the more you have something to promote, and the easier it is to get eyes on or back on your podcast. You want people to continue thinking about your podcast, hearing about your podcast, and talking about your podcast as often as possible so that you become etched in their memory. This way, if you do decide to go to a slower-paced output frequency, people still have plenty of content to listen to, and they know and like you enough to be patient for your new content to come out.

DON'T Drop the Ball on Your Promotional Activities

Even after you launch your podcast, you still need to be ready to engage in promotional activities. SEO is an extremely important tool you should be using, in particular, when it comes to promoting your strategies as SEO is how you increase your likelihood of being found. SEO strategies will work on Google, as well as search engines such as the very distribution platforms you are hosting your podcast on. If you rank well when people search for new podcasts in your niche, you will be more likely to come up over anyone else. You can increase SEO by using keywords, filling out the details of your episodes on every episode, and creating high-quality promotional materials on other platforms that direct back to your podcast. Getting featured on high-ranking websites and having them link to your podcast is also a great way to increase your SEO rankings.

It is extremely important to use timing to your advantage. You can do this by checking with other successful podcasts and seeing what their uploading patterns look like. What time of day are they generally uploading at? If you notice a pattern, use this to help you create your own uploading pattern, too, by uploading at those times of the day. Over time, your show will have enough data of its own, which will allow you to see when people are consuming your content most, so that you can upload new content when people are most likely to listen to it. The sooner you get a higher number of viewers, the better your podcast will rank, and the more viewers you will accumulate over the coming hours and days.

Another great promotion you can use is to make shareable content. Taking snippets from your show and turning them into tiny videos that can be shared online, or taking quotes from your show and turning them into pictures that can be shared online, are great ways for you to share your content out as far as possible. You can share this content on your social media platforms, with your email list, and anywhere else where you might be able to access a new audience. However, make sure you are following anti-spam practices to avoid having people think that you, and your podcast, are spamming them. You want it to come across as genuine, authentic and engaged. It is a good idea to turn this snippet-sharing process into a strategy by sharing a few clips in the days leading up to the release of your new episode. Play around with dropping these clips to see what times your audience is most receptive, then continue to share your clips at those times. Sharing a clip or two each day on the days leading up to your new episode releases ensures that you always have high quality content to share, and that said content is growing interest and excitement with your audience. This way, they will be far more likely to listen when you launch the show.

Lastly, make sure you are not writing paragraphs upon paragraphs of content about your show. People like podcasts because they don't want to be reading too much, and you need to keep that up across your digital promotions, too. Write small captions and posts and link snippets of your podcast or quote pictures into those posts. This way, people can quickly look at it, determine if they like it, tune in, and share it if they are impressed.

Make sure that you use every single place imaginable to your advantage to find new listeners. Share these posts out to Facebook groups, blogs, Reddit, and Quora. Join conversations that are relevant to your podcast and share relevant podcast episodes whenever you can. This way, people who are curious about content relevant to what you are creating will find you and listen to your show. Always be transparent when you market your podcast in this way, too, so that people are aware of the fact that you are self-promoting, as they will appreciate you being transparent more than they will appreciate you link-dropping and pretending it was a "random episode" you found. Be honest, have fun, and let your passion shine, and you will be far more likely to grow a wide listenership for your podcast.

7

HOW TO BRING YOUR PODCAST TO THE IMMEDIATE ATTENTION OF HUNDREDS, THEN THOUSANDS OF EAGER LISTENERS

There is an ocean of people trying to get noticed in the podcasting community, and each one of them is fighting to stand out more than the rest. Every method you can think of has been used in an effort to get in front of your audience so your competitors can have their podcasts heard, as they want the same success you are aiming for. If you are going to generate success with your own podcast, you need to know how to promote it properly so you can get massive attention on your podcast as soon as possible.

I want to make one thing very clear to you right now: your passion *matters*. There is a world full of people trying to get in front of every audience imaginable, including yours. They are all pounding pavement, showing themselves in the faces of their audiences, and doing everything they can to earn their attention and loyalty. Do you know what happens when you pound pavement and force yourself in front of people? *They tune you out.* Think about it... do you like it when people are hollering in your face from every angle, and trying to get you to pay attention to them? Probably not. At best, you ignore them. At worst, you get annoyed and possibly even quite angry toward them. Don't be that person. That person is only in it for one thing: money.

Be the person that is in it for passion. Host a podcast because you love doing it, because it is fun, and because you are wildly passionate about what you are talking about. Host your podcast because it is something you genuinely want to be doing, and not because you feel like this is the only way to stay relevant. When you host your podcast, be the kind of person who's energy speaks for them, and let everything else fall into place with *ease.*

It may sound challenging, but it is a lot more simple than you think. There are hundreds, if not thousands of people out there doing it successfully right now, and not one of them is forcing their way in front of a crowd and demanding their attention and loyalty. They are all sitting back, enjoying themselves, having fun, and presenting themselves and their podcasts to the people who are most likely to be interested. The entire energy is different, and it works to *attract* an audience, rather than *demand* an audience. In the end, these are the podcasters

who have thousands, if not millions of obsessed fans
who listen to every single episode they ever put out.

Bring the Market to Your Podcast

Bringing the market to your podcast means that you
pour your heart and soul into making your podcast the
best podcast possible through the power of your passion,
and then you make it possible for people to see your
podcast. A great way to think about this process would
be to think about a car. Imagine you were passionate
about sports cars, and you wanted to enjoy the experience of owning and caring for a sports car. Because of
your passion, you would likely take your time, find a
beautiful car, and take great pride in it to the point where
it is always clean and shiny, and it possibly has a few
upgrades that make it look even fancier. Your passion for
your car shows. Every time you drive down the street
(present it), people turn their heads. You did not demand
them to turn their heads by yelling out the car window
screaming at them to pay attention or by honking your
horn obsessively until they started paying attention.
Instead, you simply took pride in it, poured your passion
into it, and presented it. The attention you gained was a
natural reflection of the passion and energy you poured
into it.

This is precisely what you need to do with your podcast. You need to pour so much passion and energy into it that when it comes to marketing, the only purpose of your marketing is to present it, so your audience has the chance to see it. The quality speaks for itself, so there is no reason for you to jam that concept down everyone's throats. In order for this to really work, though, you need to make sure your promotion posts pour just as much passion into your project as your actual recordings do, too. Create graphics or share snippets from each episode that highlight the passion you have poured into your podcast, and invite people to become a part of that. They won't be able to help themselves; they will become so curious that they quite literally turn their head to see your advertising. Or, at least, they scroll back up on their phones or pause on their desktops to see what is being advertised to them.

One of the most important things to understand about promoting through passion this way is that an advertising budget is optional. Of course, if you can afford to pour money into an advertising budget and get your content out there faster, this is a great way to push your podcast up through the rankings and get as far as you possibly can. If, however, you cannot afford to put any money toward advertising, you can still market through passion and make an incredible impact with your promotions. By sharing your promotional posts in as many locations as you can and encouraging your audience to share it, too, you become far more likely to get your content out there. Again, your passion will shine through, and you *will* be heard above the crowd.

Advertise Your Podcast Efficiently

Aside from letting your passion speak for you, there are many efficient methods you can use to help get your podcast out for the world to see. These practical steps are excellent for spreading the news about your podcast, increasing your listenership, and gaining traction as your podcast continues to grow. It is important that, in order to grow your podcast as large as possible, you leverage the power of *efficient* marketing. Working smarter, not harder, gets your content out there so your audience can see it and fall in love with your show.

Efficient advertising means taking as few steps as possible to reach as many people as possible, and that these are the only methods you are focusing on. When you find methods that are not working, you should cease using them immediately. Pour your energy into the things that work.

There are four excellent methods you can use when it comes to getting a bigger audience for your page, and these methods are effortless to complete. If you pour your energy into these methods, you will be far more likely to grow your audience and get a greater listener-ship for your page.

The first method you can use to efficiently advertise your business and bring the market to you is paid advertising. Facebook and Instagram offer prestigious marketing opportunities which allow you to get yourself in front of a much larger audience as fast as possible, without having to do anything yourself. Instead, your money is working for you. On Facebook, the best advertisement would be one that features a quote from your podcast shown on an image, with a short 1-2 sentence description of your show and a link for listening. On Instagram, a short audio clip of your show pasted over an image of your show's logo or a snapshot from you recording your show would work excellently. With either platform, adequate targeting is imperative. You need to identify what your likely demographic is for your audience and define that in your advertisement's creation. If you are not entirely sure who is listening, yet, choose the most likely gender that would listen to you, or both, and then choose the most likely age group(s) that would listen to you. Then, choose a fairly narrow geographical region, such as *just* your country where you currently live. You can always target larger later, but going any larger now will result in you struggling to get a wide enough reach since it is unlikely that you have a budget that can reasonably support that large of an audience. It is important that, while you target your audience, you define a few interests your audience has that are relevant to your podcast. You could also search for some of the major podcasts in your niche to see if they come up as interests, and tag them if you can. This gives Facebook or Instagram a clear description of who you are trying to get in front of and ensures your ads are seen by people who are most likely to enjoy your content.

The most successful advertisements for podcasts have been episode clips with promotional videos attached to them, in the design of a trailer. Alternatively, an image of yourself as the host, and any other hosts of your show if you have multiple, works as this helps place a face with your podcast. The image of yourself either as an introduction to the host, or in the trailer, should be full of personality so people are immediately interested and want to learn more.

Google uses the same steps for targeting followers for your show, though it is not always the most practical method for advertising podcasts, especially newer ones, as it requires larger budgets and relies on excellent wording to grow your following. If you have a lower budget or cannot create a captivating enough written summary for your podcast, it would be best to rely on Facebook or Instagram for your podcast advertisements.

If you do have a large budget of at least $500+ and the ability to summarize your podcast in a captivating manner, then Google is an excellent place to promote your podcast, too.

The second step for growth is to get on Instagram and find people in your industry who are successful and well-respected, with the same audience you have. They can be fellow podcasters, or they can be other members of authority in your industry. Go through their followers and start engaging with their followers using comments primarily, with a few likes here and there. Follow any of the accounts that look as though they would enjoy listening to your podcast. Those followers will take notice, and if they like your account, they will follow you back. If someone does follow you back, send them a thank you message for their follow and to introduce them to your podcast in that message. You can also let them know there are a few clips on your page to give them a taste of what you have to offer, in case they want to check that out before committing to an entire episode. This is a great way to gain followers, engage with them, and turn them into actual listeners for your podcast. To optimize your conversion rate, go to that person's page, find their first name (typically by either working it out from their username or their bio), and use that when addressing them as it is far more personalized than a generic introduction, or using their username in place of their name (and also that you're not one of these pesky bots!). After a few days, unfollow any account that did not follow you back and then start again.

The third method for growing your audience is using every single place on the internet to your advantage so that you can find as many potential listeners as possible. Get on blogs, Facebook groups, Reddit and Quora, and find conversations that are relevant to your industry. Get involved in those conversations, offer your answers, and let people know you have a podcast episode that answers those questions, or that you have an upcoming episode that answers those questions. This is not only going to show the original poster your podcast but will also show every other person who had the same question and was looking for an answer, too. Getting yourself out there as much as possible, and doing so in a way that respects the user guidelines of the community, is an imperative part of growing your podcast through social networking.

Harnessing the Power of Networking

Never underestimate the power of growing your network. Networking is hands down one of the most impactful marketing strategies you will ever tap into, especially when it comes to growing your audience with a system of loyal followers. Your network will significantly boost your show by offering you many different opportunities that you simply could not create on your own. The caveat is that you need to be prepared to give back to your network as much as, if not more than, you receive from it. That is how you tap into the abundance of opportunities and grow your audience large enough for your network to genuinely support your podcast. This may sound like a lot of work, but networking is a non-negotiable when you are growing your podcast or any other platform for that matter.

"Your network is your net worth." – Porter Gale. Your network can offer you the ability to grow your podcast rapidly. You can appear as a guest on different shows, host guests on your show, and get featured in prominent marketing areas, just through knowing the right people. For example, if you build out your network and someone within your network happens to run a highly successful blog, they may wish to talk about your podcast on their blog, which earns you direct access to their major audience. In return, it is important that you support them in having plenty of high-quality pieces of content to add to their blog so you are well-represented and their audience receives the high-quality content they have become accustomed to.

Networking with other podcasters is an excellent marketing tool to exploit because it gets you in front of their audience, too, and the fact that you are a guest on their show means their audience is similar to yours. As soon as their followers listen to you, if they like you, they will seek out your podcast and become active listeners of your podcast, too. This works vice versa, too. The more you bring visitors onto your show, the more they will bring their audience with them, and your listenership will grow. This works both ways, as well, since you will also be turning your listener's attention to other podcasters, meaning they will be growing their audience, too. This creates an excellent win-win situation! It is important to have other podcasters in your network, but expand beyond them and find others' relevant to your industry, too. This expands your opportunities even further by connecting you with people who are passionate about the same things as you are but fulfilling those passions in different ways.

As you grow your network, ensure that you consider reality alongside strategy. Many times, people get caught up in the idea of using their network as a tool to leverage their growth, to the point where they routinely fail to stop and consider whether or not they actually enjoy the network they are building. Always be protective of your time and energy, even when you are investing in the growth of your podcast. You came here to do something you are passionate about, and that should leak into every aspect of your growth. If you realize that you do not mesh well with certain people in your network, do not be afraid to invest less energy in those relationships. Do not abruptly cut them out, but invest less energy over time so that the connection slowly fades. Structure your network in a way that feels like you are building a circle of friends around you who understand and share in a common interest of yours, whether it be podcasting or the specific industry you are addressing with podcasting. It should feel fun and exciting to hang out with your network of people. If it doesn't, you need to detox your network.

As far as your audience goes, your network has the capacity to turn friends and members of your network into loyal fans of your show. Likewise, you will probably also become a fan of many of theirs, too. It is important to nurture these relationships even more, as these individuals are likely to become major champions of your content. Chances are, they will share your content out, celebrate you, talk you up to their friends and family, and help get you in front of your target audience. This is because they know in return, you will offer them excellent attention and support, as well.

The best way to nurture your network is to always do your best to genuinely get to know each person in your network. Then, anytime you can offer them the same opportunities that you yourself would love to receive from your network. If you hear of opportunities that you think people in your network would fit well in, recommend them for that position, or let them know about it. Always spread the opportunities around to your network, as this ensures that you are all winning as often as possible. It also means they will be far more likely to recommend opportunities to you later, too. This also helps grow your reputation, making you the person that people love to talk about and recommend because they genuinely enjoy your generous and caring personality. It is important to understand that, in networking, you get what you give. Just like you cannot expect friends to carry your friendships as you coast by without contributing anything, you cannot expect your network to give you opportunities as you coast by without offering anything back. When you give abundantly to your network, you receive abundantly, too - like in all aspects of life, actually.

The more you contribute to your network, the more they are going to support you in growing your podcast, too. Together, you will all rise much faster. Even though you may be going at something alone, or with just one or two partners, you can still enlist the support of tens or hundreds of people, while offering support back to those individuals, too. Build your network like a strong community around you, and that network will support you in every way imaginable.

8

BUILDING YOUR BRAND: HELPING YOU STAND OUT IN THE VAST OCEAN THAT IS PODCASTING

Branding is an essential part of any business, whether it is intended to be a professional business or a hobby outlet. Podcasting is no different. If you want to stand out in the ocean of podcasters and get yourself noticed faster, you need to have a brand that is as unique as you are, and it needs to be as memorable as possible, too. By now, branding is a well-understood concept, and the steps that are required to make a stand-out brand are well-known by marketing experts. I have gone to the very sources of these marketing and branding experts and brought forward only the best tips to help you brand like a pro. In doing this, you will stand apart from everyone else. The best part is, these strategies are incredibly simple and will serve as a crucial driving factor behind your podcast becoming a success.

~

When it comes to branding like a pro, there are three main areas you need to focus on: emotional familiarity, a distinct presence, and an invaluable audience relationship. If you can create these three factors through your brand, your brand will start with a solid foundation that allows it to explode with growth as you continue to pour your energy into building your podcast.

Creating Emotional Familiarity Through Visuals

Branding guides frequently highlight the importance of having a coherent brand kit with defined colors, fonts, a well-created logo, and certain graphic themes. While this is part of it, if you rely exclusively on this information for building your brand, you will be building a brand that is superficial and disconnected from the root of what your audience really wants. True branding is not *just* about how your company looks; it is also about how your company persona is represented. Your appearance is just a part of that.

Branding is not the process of putting together a coherent, color-coded brand with consistency across your fonts and images. Those steps are all tools that you use to create the more important aspect of branding, which is emotional familiarity developed through the power of visuals. Pause for a moment and think of Coca Cola.

What comes to mind? Maybe the color red, the infamous white scripted font, the cuddly white pandas, or the sodas with your name on them. Dig deeper, though. I'll bet you also get a feeling associated with the branding, even if you are not an avid supporter of the brand itself. Maybe you get a feeling of comfort, relaxation, and community. Perhaps you feel a sense of cuteness or warmth in your heart when you think about the little panda bears. It is likely that some sort of positive feeling that washes over you anytime you think about this brand. The same can be accomplished by thinking about any major brand. That is not because they have a coherent, color-coordinated brand, but because they have developed their brand in a way that generates emotional familiarity.

Yes, you need to pick colors, fonts, a logo, and decide on a theme of what your pictures will look like so that when you post everything, it looks coherent. All of that, however, should be used to encourage your audience to feel the way you want them to feel when they think about your brand. Do you want them to feel empowered? Curious? Comfortable? Seen? Cared for? Entertained? Happy? Define some feelings you want your audience to feel every time they look at your brand. Then, choose colors that are known to encourage those feelings, fonts that match that energy, and graphics that create an emotional familiarity with those unique emotions. This will become your well-designed brand, which is not only coherent and uniformed but developed in a way that actually stands out from everyone else. The easiest way to choose your colors and design is to research what feelings are associated with the colors you are using, so you can leverage the right emotions through your brand colors. It is important, too, that these colors look neat together as you want a simple yet eye-catching brand that is different and unique from everything else. All of your branding imagery should have that same overall look to it so that you have a cohesive, attractive brand.

Developing a Distinct Online Presence

Creating a distinct online presence is an absolute must if you are going live with your podcast. You need your own website, as well as a presence on the major social media platforms. Your website is a non-negotiable when it comes to running a podcast. While you could go for a hosted website on a site building platform, I advise you to go self-hosted with WordPress. The reasoning behind this is simple: it is a bare-basics platform that has everything you need, it is fully customizable, and it will support your growth better than any other platform. Hosts like Site Ground or Host Gator can be used to host your website online, and then you can download a simple theme for your platform, or you can use a click-

and-build plugin like Divi or Elementor to build your page in an even easier manner. Your website is important because it is a hub where you can share your podcast, capture emails, and actually own the entire platform you are creating.

Your website should contain archives of your previous posts, SEO in your posts to encourage Google to show-case you to new listeners, and a comment section on your posts so listeners can interact with you. You should also have an excellent home page that acts as a landing site for you to drive promotional traffic to from your Google, Facebook, or Instagram advertisements. Your home page should include a captivating image about your show, a bio about yourself and a host image, and a directory for where your page visitors can find your posts with your episodes.

Social media is a powerhouse when it comes to developing your online presence. Social media platforms' sole focus is to attract users, and they want to connect those users with other users or brands that they are likely to enjoy. As soon as you launch an account, you can start making content, and those platforms will work to connect you with potential viewers. This is a vital step in driving traffic to your podcast, as well as to your website. Your end goal should *always* be to get people to your website, then to your podcast. However, you can encourage people to skip your website and go straight to your podcast as well, to increase your listenership. It is essential that you drive traffic to your website as often as possible though, and that you capture emails because your email captures are important. Email captures are those opt-in sections where visitors can input their emails so they can receive promotional emails from you, and they are one of the best promotional tools out there. Through your newsletter you can promote your show, find guests, and get feedback on what types of content do best for your podcast. On social media, algorithms are constantly changing, and this can be a tumultuous experience for your brand. Some changes will be excellent and will drive greater traffic your way, while other changes will be difficult and could actually take traffic away from your content. At times, when platforms are down completely, you can lose total access to your audience, which results in you not being able to promote your podcast and keep your listenership up. This has happened a couple of times within the last five years, so recognize that this is a real possibility, and it can throw a damper into your business. If you own your website and have an email capture, however, you can still access your listeners even when social media is down, which means you are not required to start from scratch and work your way back up from ground zero.

As you develop your presence on your website and social media, incorporate your branding elements, so everything looks coherent and uniform. Then, take it a massive step further. Look at the emotional aspects of everything you post and ask yourself if those aspects match the emotional familiarity you want to be creating with your brand. Everything from the imagery to the words you are using should match that emotional tone, while also clearly reflecting your purpose and driving traffic to your page, your website, or your podcast. If you are unsure about how a post fits your brand, pause before posting it, and give yourself time to think about it. This way, you get it right the first time. You never want to find yourself in a situation where you post content in a leap decision because you just want to get it out there, only to find yourself thinking of a much better way to say it later on and not being able to go fix it because it has already been put out. Taking your time and creating high-quality, well-branded content the first time ensures that your content spreads farther, makes a greater impact, and grows your podcast exactly the way you desired it would. Remember, you want to work smarter, not harder. Every post you make should reflect your distinct, stand-out brand; otherwise, it should not be posted.

$\sim$

Cultivating an Invaluable Audience Relationship

The relationship you build with your audience will help you stand apart from the crowd by making you memorable. Think about the last time you went and met a group of new people. Perhaps you went to a party, a meeting, or some other gathering and noticed that there were many new faces there. Out of all of the people you met that day, I bet one or two people stood out in particular. Why? Because in that time, there was a relationship built, even if it was only an acquaintanceship, and it made a lasting impression. Anyone who you did not get the chance to make any form of connection with, you have likely already forgotten about.

When your audience comes onto any social media platform, you want to be the one putting the energy into developing a relationship with them so that you are the one they remember. This relationship should not be a sleazy strategy you use for self-fulfillment, either. The relationship you build with your audience needs to be founded on passion, mutual interest, and a genuine desire to come together and connect over something you both find meaningful. Your number one focus should be on *real* relationships, not just fake or superficial relationships you create in an effort to grow your podcast.

Understand that as you cultivate these relationships, your audience will know right away if your "relationship-building tactics" are a sham you are using to grow your podcast. Everyone else is using these very same lame, surface-level tactics to build fake relationships with their audience so they can loosely back up the claim that they "care." Their potential audience already knows, however, they are not doing this because they desire real relationships, they are doing this because they desire a following and they need that audience to listen to their podcast in order to gain that following. It feels weak, greedy, and frustrating. Their potential audience feels used instead of connected with, and so they stop listening. Whether you realize it or not, every audience is growing increasingly more sensitive to fake relationship-building tactics that brands are using. They can smell the fake from a mile away, and they are steering clear of it. In fact, if you reflect on brands you have interacted with, you can likely recall ones that were alarmingly fake, too.

This is where we tie back into the reality that passion has to be the foundation of your podcast before anything else. Even if you want to make money, gain clout, or do anything else beyond following your passion, these desires must always be second to your desire to fulfill your passion. Otherwise, you will never have the energy to invest in doing the things that will actually make you grow. For example, making real relationships with your audience.

Creating a real relationship with your audience comes from being passionate enough to recognize repeat listeners and spend a few extra moments liking their comments, commenting back, and engaging with them in a genuine manner. Your real relationships are developed by caring about what your audience wants and creating more of it, and by genuinely receiving their feedback and using it to improve the quality of your show. At the core of your relationships should always be what you would offer to any relationship in your personal life, except that you are striving to offer it in a broader way. Be honest, trustworthy, and loyal to your following, and they will be open and loyal with you, too. Use listener recognition, contests, giveaways, shout outs, and daily attention as a way to give back to your followers. In return, they will passionately give back to you by sharing your podcast with everyone they know.

9

THE FOOLPROOF RECIPE FOR LONG TERM SUCCESS

When you initially start your podcast, it can be easy to get caught up in the beginning stages and forget about the fact that after you launch your podcast, you have to keep going in order to succeed. Yes, those early episodes and initial listeners are important, but after those first couple of months, you need to have a strategy to keep you consistent and motivate you to go after that long-term success. If you are not in it for the long-run, you will not receive all of the benefits that podcasting has to offer. Further, if you cannot picture yourself doing this for the long-run, you may not be pursuing your passion at all, and you may want to reconsider or adjust your podcast to ensure it matches your desires. If you are confident that this is what you want, maintain a long-term mindset, stay consistent, and use the greatest source of motivation most podcasters are sleeping on, which I will reveal to you in just a moment...

Maintaining a Long-Term Mindset

A long-term mindset means that you have a mindset that is prepared to remain committed to your success for the long-term, even when you come up against adversity such as worldly events, life circumstances, or even your own lack of attention. Humans, in general, have an incredibly challenging time maintaining a long-term mindset because they want to be fulfilled by instant gratification. If that instant gratification is not fulfilled, they lose interest. Or, worse, that feeling of gratification is fulfilled by launching the podcast, but then it seems pointless afterward because it seems like they have already "fulfilled their desires." Of course, they likely wanted much more out of their podcast than just that, but their lack of long-term mindset leaves them feeling like they are "already done."

Creating a long-term mindset is key to creating longevity for your podcast. You can create it by developing a willingness to repeat the same process over and over, without seeing any significant or jaw-dropping results from your efforts. Instead, you will see small cumulative growth over time, and eventually, that will turn into significant results. You also need to be willing to motivate yourself to keep going, even when you feel challenged, bored, or distracted. Eliminate your desire to become obsessed with incredible results, and focus instead on connecting with your desire to do something you are passionate about and to have a long-term outlet to channel that passion through.

How You Can Stay Consistent

Consistency determines how successful your podcast will, or will not be. It is easy to maintain consistency at first because your podcast is exciting and new, so you are eager to record new episodes and get them up on your show. Over time, however, this excitement drops and you may find yourself less excited because the novelty has worn off. While your podcast does not require round the clock care, it is important that you learn to channel your excitement into a consistent routine so that as the novelty does begin to wear off, you find yourself still readily available to keep the show going.

Right from the start, develop a schedule that you can eagerly follow with your show. Your schedule should include when you will be recording your shows, when you will be editing them, and when you will be uploading them. In your schedule, aim to batch content so that you can record multiple shows at once, edit multiple shows at once, and upload multiple shows into your host at once. You should be able to schedule shows within your host platform so they do not go live to the public until a specific time and date, which ensures that your episodes are ready to go well in advance of their actual release date. The release date should be the only portion of your schedule that you advertise to your audience, though you can use small videos and clips of the "behind the scenes" parts of your schedule, including recording and editing, as a way to promote your podcast.

Aside from a schedule, a routine is excellent for your consistency, too. A routine defines what you do once you are planning and writing shows, in the recording studio, editing software, or at the uploading or promotional phases. Your routine defines what you do, when, and how each session goes, and it should be developed in a way that maximizes your efficiency while ensuring that the same things are completed each time. For example, during the planning and writing phase, your routine might include brainstorming your show, picking out the best parts of your brain storm, fitting them into a pre-made outline for how your show goes, and then writing the first draft. Then, you can edit your writing, read it over, test it out, and edit it once more. This type of routine ensures your show is always well-written, contains plenty of exciting content, and has the same flow in every episode.

You can increase your consistency, too, by increasing your confidence and expanding your capacity to stay motivated. The easiest way to do this is by writing down your small achievements every single day, whether it be completing a new episode, gaining more listeners, or receiving a nice comment from a listener. As you realize how much success you are creating with your show, you will find it easier to maintain confidence and keep going because you realize that the effort you are putting into your show is paying off. When you start to see how well-received you and your show are, it becomes easier to motivate yourself to keep going.

The Greatest Source of Motivation That the Majority of Podcasters Sleep on

There is a specific source of motivation that everyone can tap into that most podcasters are not taking advantage of. This source of motivation can explode your confidence, increase your desire to pursue your success, and stay focused on creating the podcast of your dreams. It is a source that virtually everyone experiences, too. That is: feedback from your audience.

So many podcasters are so focused on themselves and what they are doing that they forget to stop and listen to their audience. Rather than truly hearing their audience celebrating their efforts and praising their content, they stay focused on what is happening directly in front of them. That may be the latest course, book, trend, or to-do list that needs to get done. Whatever it is, it is taking their attention away from a powerful motivator that can give you the energy to keep going, while also making you feel entirely fulfilled for everything you have already achieved.

Every single day, stop and listen to the positive feedback from your audience. Let it resonate with you. Take it in. And, let it guide you for where to go next. Stick to a schedule and put out content, as this will keep everyone else on your schedule and spending time with you, too. Plus, a schedule will keep you consistent. The more you adhere to your own schedule, the more your listeners will too, and the bigger your podcast will grow. Don't just schedule your episodes, schedule all of the tasks that go into producing and marketing your episodes, too. Then, listen to all of the great feedback you are receiving and let it sink in deep, giving you the motivation you need to keep going.

10

HOW TO TURN YOUR HOBBY INTO INCOME

Finally, if you are wondering how you can turn your podcast into an income, we are there! Creating an income stream from your podcast is easier than you think, and you can actually start this process as soon as you have the foundations of a community centered around your podcast. Once you have a steady audience listening to your content week in week out, you can start monetizing your show so you can earn money, too!

7 Streams of Income

Let the seven streams of income theory sink into your mindset before you get started with any monetization strategies. The seven streams of income theory are that all millionaires have at least seven successful income streams, and those income streams are directly responsible for building their wealth. They start with building one source of wealth, master it, and then move on to the next one. Once they master that, they do it all over again until they have at least seven consistent income streams. Sure enough, it works every time.

This theory is important for your podcast because it helps remind you not to put your eggs in one basket. There are many opportunities you have for monetizing your show and earning cash from your podcast. You need to be willing to keep your mind open and search for as many different methods as possible, but it is important that you master each method before moving on to the next so that you build in a concise, simple manner. If you try to rush it, you might overwhelm yourself, fail miserably, and possibly sabotage your reputation in the process. Be patient, sure-footed, and consistent, and you will get results.

Seven excellent streams of income you can tap into with your podcast include: affiliate marketing, sponsorships, selling merch, monetizing your content, selling intellectual property, hosting events, content marketing, or receiving donations from listeners - easily done using Patreon or other subscription platforms.

How to Construct the Perfect Email That WILL Get Sponsors Running Your Way

The number one method for getting income through your podcast is through getting sponsors. Sponsors are individuals who pay you to create a podcast episode. More specifically, they pay you to talk about them throughout your podcast episode. A sponsor will generally ask you to talk about their business at the beginning, middle, and end of the show. At the beginning, it is often introduced by saying, "Today's show is sponsored by ___." And then quickly introducing the company. Then, halfway through the show, you can share another piece of information about the show, and at the end of the show, you can create a call to action for your sponsor.

Getting sponsors can be accomplished by first creating a consistent listenership. Then, you need to create the perfect email to pitch your show to potential sponsors so that they consider sponsoring your show. The perfect sponsorship email should be written in three parts: the introduction, the pitch, and the call to action.

Before you ever send a sponsorship request letter to a brand, you need to make contact with that brand, build a relationship with them, and increase your rapport. You should never make a sponsorship your first point of contact with a brand, as this guarantees you will experience extremely low success rates in your ability to receive sponsorships. Instead, warm them up using a letter that introduces who you are, thanks them for their product, and establishes a connection between yourself and the brand. Never talk about financial requests, samples of your ability, pictures of your stakeholders or users, need for their sponsorship, generic wording, or assumptions about who their target audience is.

After you have spent some time building rapport, either by complementing their products, thanking them for making excellent products, or by asking for tips on how to make better use of products, you can send a sponsorship letter.

Your sponsorship letter needs to include five key pieces of information: an introduction, the reason you got in touch, information about your audience, your sponsorship opportunities, and a mention of when you will follow up with them.

Your introduction should not be a long-winded explanation of who you are, what your podcast is about, what your mission and vision are, and everything else. Instead, it should be a brief 2-3 sentence summary of who you are and what your podcast is about.

Your reason for getting in touch should explain why you chose their specific company, *not* a request for financial sponsorship. Make it clear as to why this particular company was the best for you to use, what you appreciate about their brand, and why you thought the two of you should meet. Create commonalities here by identifying where your common goals align and why you think your audience would love their products or services.

Your information about your audience needs to include details on who your audience is and why you feel they would like the product you are requesting to be sponsored for. Never assume you know who the brand's target audience is, but do explain why you feel your audience is a part of their target audience. Never leave data about your audience out of the pitch, or you will be leaving money on the table.

Your sponsorship opportunity should explain how you plan on sponsoring those products so you can increase sales for that company. You should include three methods for how you will promote them in a way that your audience will love, and that will earn them higher sales through your show. Explain information about branding, sampling, product placements, or even contests you would run to promote their products.

Lastly, you need to let them know when you will follow up so they know when to hear back from you. This is important as it shows you are serious about working together, and it sets the intention that follow up will be sent off. This way, your sponsor does not think you are spamming their inbox, because you are actually just following up on a promise you made in a prior email when you email them again at a later date.

Getting Income Streams Through Your Podcast

Aside from sponsors, you can make money through other streams with your podcast, too. Podcasters often make money through selling products or services and using their podcasts to advertise them, affiliate marketing, crowdfunding, virtual summits, events, and premium content. All of these different income streams should always be developed in a way that clearly fits your industry, and that fits perfectly with your podcast, and brand. Never advertise something that is irrelevant to your podcast. Even if you think you have the right audience, if it is irrelevant, it will turn out poor results. That is not why your audience comes to you. Further, they may start to judge you or resent you for making them feel like all you want to do is sell to them. In worst-case scenarios, it may confuse your audience and drive them away, and these hiccups could make getting into your next sponsorship or income stream method even more challenging.

When you do begin adding income streams through your podcast, make sure you take your time, thoughtfully develop each income stream, and introduce it in a positive and meaningful way. Especially with your first one, take time to create a grand opening around the introduction of this new income stream if it is a product or service you are creating and selling, and get your audience excited about it. Always give everyone time to get used to each new income stream being added to your show, as you want them to have an opportunity to become familiar with it, interact with it, and ultimately purchase before you move on to the next opportunity. If you pack too many on at once, you might overwhelm or confuse your audience. Be patient, be persistent, and be passionate about everything you do, and your audience will always happily accept your advancements.

CONCLUSION

Congratulations on completing *Podcasting Made Simple!* This podcasting book was designed to help you launch your dream podcast, have a blast doing it, and possibly earn some money if you wish to monetize your podcast. By now, you have everything you need to feel confident launching your very own podcast!

Podcasting may not be a brand new medium, but it is one that is certainly growing in popularity. As it does, there is still a window of opportunity for new podcasters to jump on board and make a killing off their shows. However, there is no telling how long that window will remain open, so you need to get started with launching your podcast *right now*. There is no more time to waste!

Before you leave this book, I want to make sure that you feel rock solid on the foundation you require in order to build the next viral podcast. It starts with having a clear vision and having a great amount of passion in that vision. Never pursue a podcast that you are not absolutely passionate about, because you will not have the energy that you need to get people interested, keep your show going, and work through the challenges you will face along the way. Your passion will bring a level of energy to your voice and approach that is unparalleled, and that cannot be faked.

Once you have a foundation of passion, you need to focus on the logistics. While passion, energy, and relationships are at the core of your success, you also need to have high-quality podcasting supplies to keep you going. Focus on getting the best microphone you can afford, get yourself somewhere nice and quiet where you can record your episodes, and learn how to produce your episodes using basic editing strategies. Don't forget your signature intro or outro, as they are an important part of building the emotion and making your show a memorable one!

With the logistics figured out, you can focus all of your energy into creating episodes, building relationships with your audience, and using efficient marketing strategies to get your episodes to your audience. Always, *always* choose efficient marketing strategies, as they allow you to work smarter not harder. The best way to use the most efficient marketing strategies available is to research trending marketing strategies and begin using them in your business. Then, pay close attention to what is working and what isn't, and ditch anything that is not moving significant engagement around your platforms. Focus only on that which is really driving traffic your way.

It may take some time to build momentum around your podcast, even if you chose an elaborate grand opening strategy, and that is okay. I encourage you to tap into that passion that got you here in the first place and to focus on nothing other than creating shows filled with that passionate energy. Once you have your shows consistently flowing, learn to pour that passion into fun and effective marketing strategies, and trust that one of them is going to hit it big and bring you an audience. If you have the budget, you can also use paid advertisements to increase your marketing efforts and bring the audience to you. Even without a budget, make sure you always execute attraction marketing strategies as they will help you stand out.

Before you ever publish anything, whether it is an episode or a piece of promotional material, make sure you always review it to ensure it has the right energy and invokes the right emotions. You want to inspire happiness, curiosity, inspiration, passion, and excitement in your audience as much as possible. The more you can generate positive, meaningful associations between your podcast and your audience, the more they will tune in and listen to everything you have to say. This is how you create an audience full of loyal listeners who listen to every episode you launch and share all your best episodes with their friends.

Of course, don't forget about the value of relationships, either. You need to nurture the relationships with your audience and with your network so that you can experience all of the support you need to build your circle and keep it growing. With your audience, focus on building a strong parasocial relationship by caring for them, showing gratitude for their presence, and inviting them to engage with you. Give more than you take, focus on building relationships, and look for every way possible to add joy to the lives of your audience. Learning how to be a giving persona will make all the difference in the joy you gain from your podcast, and the loyalty you gain from your listeners.

With your network, focus on building strong relationships and always look to connect people with opportunities that would best suit them, and watch how this results in you being connected with great opportunities, too. Be generous in your relationships, and you will receive everything you want and need out of them, plus so much more. Your passion podcast can bring a great deal of fulfillment and joy to your life, if you let it.

Before you go, I ask that you please take a moment to review *Podcasting Made Simple* on Amazon Kindle. Your honest feedback would be greatly appreciated, as it will help me create more great content for you, and will help fellow podcasters get started on their own passionate journeys, too. It's a win-win situation!

Happy podcasting!

Daniel Larson

A SPECIAL OPPORTUNITY

Due to popular demand, I compiled a comprehensive 16-part video training series on how to optimize your show for growth and improve your podcast marketing through simple yet effective strategies.

The crash course takes podcasters from confused and uncertain to clear and confident on how to gain more listeners and grow their audience. As a valued reader of my book, you can access the *Podcast Marketing Kickstarter* with an 80% discount at:

https://daniel-larson.com/reader-special-offer

RESOURCE PAGE

A special thanks to sound engineer Jake Fielding for his lending me his expertise for chapter 4. Visit www.jake-fielding.com for expert production for your project.

Ciccarelli, S., *Voices,* The 4 Different Types of Podcasts. (30 October, 2019.) https://www.voices.com/blog/4-different-types-podcasts/

McLean, M., *The Podcast Host*, 7 Podcast Tips to Build a Successful Show that Thrives. (3 December, 2018) https://www.thepodcasthost.com/planning/how-to-make-a-successful-podcast/

Podcast.co, 9 Tips for Conducting Better Podcast Interviews. https://www.podcast.co/create/tips-for-better-podcast-interviews

Roth, C., *Entrepreneur,* Customer Loyalty 3.0 Is Never About Transactions. It's About Getting to Know Your Customers. (11 April, 2016.) https://www.entrepreneur.com/article/273761

Winn, R., *Podcast Insights,* Best Podcast Recording Software (For Mac & PC). (20 May, 2020.) https://www.podcastinsights.com/best-podcast-recording-software/

CPSIA information can be obtained
at www.ICGtesting.com
Printed in the USA
BVHW081015160223
658643BV00007B/172